From 1,200+ organizations trained over 15 years

$125M → $1.2B — One client has used the PRECISE Playbook for 12 years. They've grown from $125 million to $1.2 billion in annual revenue.

12x dealer revenue — A heavy equipment manufacturer installed the PRECISE Playbook as the common language for 500 distributors—professionalizing every rep with the same process.

10x revenue increase — A SaaS company replaced product-dumping with PRECISE Discovery, uncovering what prospects actually wanted to change—moving stalled deals 3x faster.

85% win rate — An insurance brokerage replaced 'checking in' with Value, Pain, and Namedrop Hooks—removing hope from their sales strategy.

300% AUM growth — An asset management firm mastered the Call Sheet, knowing more about prospects than expected—establishing presence competitors couldn't match.

18 → 9 month cycle — A healthcare EHR provider used Explore to identify hidden blockers early—doubling their implementation rate.

45% more opportunities — A global insurer required Explore for decision-makers on every call—preventing late-stage deal death.

15% higher margins — A medical device company shifted from pitching to Story → Scene → Translation—moving conversations from price to patient outcomes.

40% more closed-won — A B2B payment processor trained on SHARP to handle micro-objections—eliminating 'circling back' from their vocabulary.

Multi-year exclusives — A chemical distributor used Structured Choices to guarantee supply certainty—locking out price-focused competitors.

These outcomes are not created by training alone. They are created by behavior that stayed consistent long after training ended.

We've seen other teams attend the same workshops, learn the same frameworks, and leave with the same enthusiasm—then change nothing. Their pipelines stayed flat. Their close rates didn't move. Not because the system failed, but because adoption never happened.

The difference between the results above and the results that never came is not information. It's installation.

What Sales Leaders Are Saying

"We brought PRECISE in to do two things: fill our pipeline and sharpen our sales team. Their Performers SDR team handles our outbound prospecting with the same discipline they teach in the PRECISE Selling Playbook, which we use to train our own closers. The combination gave us a complete sales engine — expert prospecting feeding into a team that knows how to convert. Last year was the best year in Touchplan's history, and PRECISE was a big part of that."

— Richard Peasley, EVP, MOCA Systems Inc. (Touchplan)

"PRECISE Selling brings discipline and clarity to sales teams that need to perform. From a private equity perspective, their ability to professionalize sales execution and drive consistent results makes them a trusted partner in value creation."

— Chris Meyers, Partner, Hull Street Capital

"I've spent my career in high-dollar, complex sales environments. PRECISE Selling works because it teaches sales professionals how to think—how to ask better questions, uncover real needs, and navigate complicated buying decisions with confidence. It's practical, disciplined, and effective at scale. This is the kind of system serious sales organizations need."

— David Putz, Executive Vice President, Brown & Brown Insurance

"PRECISE Selling helped us build a true sales organization. The process works across experience levels, roles, and markets, and it became foundational to how we communicate, prospect, and grow. Brian understands the realities of healthcare, manufacturing, and distribution better than anyone we've worked with."

— Bill Sparks, Founder, MedPro Associates

"Partnering with Brian and PRECISE has proven incredibly beneficial to our sales organization. His engaging and relatable approach equipped our teams with practical strategies they use every day, helping drive double-digit growth and build a strong foundation for the future."
— **Matt Bruggeman, President, Ritz Safety**

"I've used PRECISE Selling across more than one company, and it consistently delivers results. The framework is practical, repeatable, and adaptable to virtually any sales cycle. It's become a foundational part of how I sell and coach sales teams."
— **Riley Van Hofwegen, CEO, Tenacore**

"PRECISE Selling isn't theory—it's a repeatable sales system that drives adoption and long-term performance. We've used it for over a decade, retrain regularly, and it continues to scale as our organization grows."
— **Steven Stolfi, President, Corsearch**

"I transitioned into a role that required me to win new accounts. Within 60 days of using PRECISE Selling, I captured a significant new account every month for the next year. Prepare, practice, and you will perform."
— **Sean Sullivan, Director of Portfolio Management, NGC**

1:00 PM on a Tuesday

Five industries. Federal intelligence. Auto Finance. Wound care. Senior living. Construction.

Seventeen meetings booked this morning. Multiple decision-makers mapped. Strategic briefings written. VPs, Directors of Nursing, and C-suite founders—all on the calendar before lunch was over.

And my team was still dialing.

This book will teach you how we do it. Then it will teach your closers how to get the deal to the finish line.

You'll see exactly how that Tuesday happened at the end of this book.

PRECISE Selling

PRECISE Selling

20 Days to the Top

The Sales Playbook for Turning
Conversations into Commitments

Brian Sullivan, CSP

PRECISE Publishing

Copyright © 2026 by Brian Sullivan, CSP

All rights reserved. No part of this publication may be reproduced, distributed, or transmitted in any form or by any means, including photocopying, recording, or other electronic or mechanical methods, without the prior written permission of the publisher, except in the case of brief quotations embodied in critical reviews and certain other noncommercial uses permitted by copyright law.

ISBN: 979-8-218-92040-1 (Paperback)

First Edition

Printed in the United States of America

Published by PRECISE Publishing

www.preciseselling.com

To my wife, Leanne—everything starts with us. You are the real leader of the Sullivan household, my partner in everything that matters, and the reason I get to do any of this. Your encouragement, honesty, and belief in me are the fuel behind everything in this book.

To my kids—Jake, Shea, and Maggie—thank you for reminding me that the most important sale I'll ever make is showing up for you. You are my favorite people.

And to my mom, Judy Sullivan, whose quiet strength, generosity, and love shaped the way I look at people and relationships. Whatever is good in how I sell and how I teach selling started with you.

Contents

The 20 Days That Will Change Your Career

Most sales books are written from the sidelines.

This one is written from the field.

Our 25-plus-person PRECISE Performer sales team makes at least 500 cold calls each week per rep, carries real quotas, and closes dozens of opportunities while protecting healthy margins in markets where connect rates sit under 5% and buyers are allergic to "just checking in." The same team then runs discovery, navigates buying groups, presents solutions, and closes deals that range from simple one-call closes to complex, multi-stakeholder enterprise sales.

At PRECISE Selling, two things matter: teaching salespeople how to become top performers, and doing it ourselves under pressure.

Nothing in this book is theory; it's the system that keeps our business—and our clients' businesses—healthy.

This book will teach you that system.

But first, you need to see why so many smart, hardworking salespeople are still stuck—and why it's not a "motivation" problem.

Why This Hurts (And Why It's Not Your Fault)

Most salespeople are winging it.

They walk into calls hoping the right words will show up. They ask questions they haven't thought through. They "explain what we do" in three confusing minutes instead of 30 seconds. They handle objections differently every time.

And when the buyer says, "Let me think about it," they send a proposal and pray.

That's not a sales process.

That's improvisation with a CRM.

Over time, it costs you pipeline, commissions, and confidence. You start to feel like some invisible force is deciding which deals close and which ones quietly die, and you're just along for the ride.

Here's the truth: you're not crazy, and you're not lazy.

Sales didn't suddenly get harder because salespeople got worse. The environment changed. Today, buyers often complete most of their decision process before speaking to a salesperson. When they finally talk to you, you're competing for a tiny slice of their total buying time, usually shared with other vendors. Decision-makers gather information from a long list of sources before giving you a real conversation.

Attention is scarce. Trust is fragile. The margin for guessing is gone.

Cold call connect rates in many industries sit below 5%. Cold email response rates often live under 1%. Decision-makers get dozens of sales touches every week and ignore most of them without a second thought.

In that environment, winging it doesn't just fail.

It never even gets noticed.

So if you've been working hard and still feel stuck, it's not because you don't care. It's because no one handed you a complete system that works in this reality, under pressure.

Why Most Training Feels Incomplete

If you've been in sales for more than a year, you've probably seen pieces of good training.

Maybe you've learned a question-based method that helps you uncover pain, an insight-driven approach that pushes you to teach instead of just "build rapport," a qualification framework that keeps you from chasing ghosts, or an account strategy model that maps the real decision-makers.

All of those are useful. Some are excellent.

But here's the gap: most of those systems were built to shine in one part of the sale.

They might help you ask better questions in discovery, qualify more rigorously, map the buying committee, or deliver sharper insights. What they don't do is run an entire conversation from the first "hello" to the commitment—especially when the pressure is on.

They rarely tell you exactly how to open a cold call so you sound like a pro in six seconds, how to sequence questions so buyers open up instead of shutting down, how to explain what you do in 30 seconds without killing curiosity, what to say when a deal slides into "I need to think about it," or how to secure clear next steps instead of "circling back" into oblivion.

So you end up juggling fragments: one framework for discovery, another for qualification, another for account strategy, another for "challenging" the customer.

Then you get on a live call. A real human with a real quota on your shoulders. The buyer throws you a curveball.

And you're not executing a system.

You're mentally flipping through a toolbox, hoping you grab the right tool in time.

That's not your fault.

You were given pieces.

You were never given the whole.

What PRECISE Is (And Isn't)

PRECISE is a complete framework—from the first cold call to the final commitment.

It works in simple, transactional sales with one decision-maker and one call. It works in mid-complexity deals with a handful of stakeholders and several meetings. It works in enterprise sales with 10–15 stakeholders, long cycles, and political landmines.

The principles don't change. Only the altitude and complexity do.

PRECISE stands for:

P – Prepare. Research and plan before the call. Know who you're talking to and why, so you don't waste their time—or yours.

R – Respect & Trust. Earn credibility in the first six seconds. Sound like a professional, not a desperate stranger.

E – Engage. Ask questions in a clear sequence to uncover real problems. Stop pitching. Start diagnosing.

C – Convey. Present your solution with a simple structure: Story → Scene → Translation. Show what matters; skip the feature parade.

I – Indecision. Handle fear and uncertainty with calm structure. Navigate "let me think about it" without pressure or panic.

S – Secure Agreement. Use structured choice at every stage. "Thursday at 10 or Friday at 2?" beats "let me know what works."

E – Explore. Identify and involve the real buying committee. Get the right people in the room early, not after six doomed meetings.

PRECISE is not a script.

It's not a trick.

It's not a shortcut.

PRECISE is a guardrail.

When pressure hits, when your mind blanks, when the buyer throws you an objection you've heard a hundred times but still hate, the framework keeps you from driving the call off a cliff.

You don't need to be perfect. You need a road you can stay on.

The 20-Day Promise

This is not a book you "read once and feel inspired by."

It's a 20-day rebuilding project for how you prepare for calls, open conversations, ask questions, present solutions, handle indecision, and secure next steps.

If you commit to the process for 20 days, your preparation will become intentional instead of last-minute browsing. Your questions will become sharper and more useful. Your conversations will feel calmer, and your deals will stall less often because next steps are clear and agreed on.

You won't become some mythic "perfect closer" in 20 days. But you will be measurably, visibly better. Your manager will notice. Your buyers will notice. You'll notice.

That's what happens when you stop guessing and start running a structure that can hold up under pressure.

One Framework, Every Level

Most sales methodologies are built for one environment. One is perfect for complex discovery. Another is great for mid-market qualification. Another shines in enterprise account strategy. They're all excellent—in their lane.

The problem is your career doesn't stay in one lane. SDRs get promoted to AEs. AEs move into enterprise. VPs try to create one language across all three and end up with three different systems that don't talk to each other.

That creates a hidden cost: every time your role or your deal complexity changes, you're back to square one with a new playbook.

PRECISE doesn't work that way.

You learn it once as an SDR making cold calls. You use the same framework as an AE running discovery and demos. You use the same framework as an enterprise seller navigating buying committees and pilots.

The questions get deeper.

The stakeholders multiply.

The timelines stretch.

The language stays the same.

That's how you build mastery—not by relearning the game every time the stakes go up, but by scaling the same system to a bigger field.

Final Word Before We Start

This isn't a motivational book.

It's a manual. A playbook. A framework you can run in real conversations with real buyers, in an environment that doesn't hand out second chances easily.

Over the next 20 days, you'll see stories, frameworks, and very specific moves. Some will confirm what you already do well. Some will contradict habits you've carried for years. A few may sting a little.

That's okay.

The goal isn't to make you feel good about where you are. The goal is to give you a repeatable way to get where you want to go.

If you're willing to be coached—whether you're an SDR, an AE, or a VP who thinks you've seen it all—turn the page.

PART I

THE FOUNDATION

CHAPTER 1

The Proctologist & The Pitch

How One Angry Doctor Shoved Me Into the Sales Hall of Pain

I learned one of the greatest lessons of my entire sales career not from a sales trainer, a motivational guru, or a bestselling book.

I learned it from a proctologist.

Yes. A proctologist.

And this was not the kind of "personal growth" experience you brag about on LinkedIn.

If you ever hear me give a keynote, you know this is how I start. Not because I enjoy emotional pain, but because this ridiculous, humiliating, completely true moment is the reason PRECISE Selling even exists.

Let's go back.

The Young Hotshot Who Thought He Knew Everything

Picture a young Sully at medical device company Welch Allyn. I was part of the new generation—the ones with energy, the ones who wanted to change the world. And I thought I was God's gift to gastroenterology sales.

Full swagger. Big smile. A colonoscope demo kit slung over my shoulder like a guitar case.

I was ready to "wow" some doctors.

Or so I thought.

The Wrong Two Doctors

I walk into this gorgeous GI practice—marble floors, water feature in the lobby, leather chairs that probably cost more than my first car. Two younger doctors greet me.

Doctor #1: tall, handsome, confident handshake, alpha male. Doctor #2: shorter, glasses slipping down his nose, looks like the guy who recalibrates ultrasound machines on weekends.

So naturally, like a rookie, I pitch the alpha.

I'm flying through features. "Illuminated tip, ergonomic control, smoother insertion—" It was like watching a blender without a lid.

I finish with my patented closer: "So... you two want one of these things?"

The tall doctor bursts out laughing. Not "Ha, that's funny," but "Oh my God, this guy's an idiot."

I ask, "Why are you laughing?"

He says, "Brian, we have no authority to make decisions in this office."

I blink. "Then who does?"

He points to the shorter doctor. "His dad."

I turn to the geeky guy. "Can you go get your dad?"

He shakes his head. "No."

"Why not?"

He looks over his glasses and says: "He hates salespeople."

"Think he'll hate me?"

He pauses. Studies my face. Lowers his voice.

"Oh... I know he'll hate you."

And that's when Dad arrives.

Enter Popeye

This man was five-foot-six of pure authority. Bald head. Forearms like Popeye after a spinach binge. A stare that could sterilize surgical tools.

He walks into the room. No greeting. No smile. Zero patience.

I spring into action. "Doctor! Brian Sullivan from Welch Allyn! Great day to show you our—" Then I blasted him with a laundry list of worthless features he had no interest in.

No reaction. He looks at me like I'm a fly buzzing around his lasagna.

So I panic-talk. Faster. Louder. More features. "Illuminated tip! Improved deflection! Flex shaft!" Pure desperation disguised as enthusiasm.

Finally, he steps closer. Crosses his arms.

And says the line:

"Son... I've looked up more assholes than you have hairs on your head."

Silence. The kind of silence that makes you rethink every decision that led to this moment.

I nervously laugh. "Ha... that was funny!"

He doesn't laugh.

He leans in and asks: "Funny how?"

This man wasn't joking. He wasn't bantering. He wasn't giving me a hard time. He was telling me: "You're an idiot, and we're going to deal with this right now."

Dragged by the Tie

He reaches out. Grabs my tie. My actual tie. And starts walking.

I stumble past nurses, patients, medical assistants—all pretending not to see what's happening.

He pulls me into his office. Shuts the door. Releases the tie. Points at the chair.

"Sit."

I sit like a grounded middle-schooler.

He paces once. Then turns and says:

"Son, let me explain something. I've been doing this for 45 years. You didn't ask me a single question about my patients, my practice, or my needs. You just talked."

Then: "You're supposed to diagnose before you prescribe. You did the opposite."

Then: "If a patient walks into my exam room, and I make a diagnosis before ever asking them questions, then asking them some more, and then listening deeply to what they were telling me, I'd probably kill somebody."

Then the dagger: "You just did the sales version of that."

I sat there, stunned.

And I realized—I deserved every second of it.

The Drive Home

I left that appointment like a dog that'd been kicked. Tie crooked. Ego bruised. Confidence leaking out my shoes.

And halfway down the highway, I learned something that would change my life forever:

Arrogance kills curiosity.

And curiosity is the foundation of great selling.

I realized that day I didn't know how to sell at all. I knew how to talk. But I didn't know how to ask. Or listen. Or diagnose. Or earn trust.

That doctor didn't hate salespeople.

He hated lazy salespeople. Ones who showed up assuming they already knew the answers.

Sound familiar? It should. It's still happening today.

The Hotel Meeting Room

A few weeks later, I'm at a regional sales meeting near O'Hare. Classic conference room: buzzing fluorescents, loud carpet, stale coffee.

Our VP of Sales, John Moran, pulls me aside after the morning session. "Brian, how are things going out there?"

I take a deep breath. "John… you're not going to believe this sales call I had."

I tell him the whole story—the two younger docs, the decision-maker who hates salespeople, the hairs-on-my-head comment, the tie grab, the humiliation.

John starts laughing so hard he nearly spills his coffee.

When he finally catches his breath, he wipes his eyes, looks at me, and says:

"Brian… that's not your fault."

I blink. Did he just say not my fault?

He continues: "We don't have a sales methodology. We don't have a process. We don't have a common language. We just throw people out into the field and say… good luck."

Then he points at me. "I want you, John Keady, and Jack DeSaro to build one."

I freeze. "You want me to build a… sales process?"

"Yes."

"Like… a real one?"

"Yes."

Then he gives the line that changed the trajectory of my career:

"Your job is simple: Take the C-players to Bs, the Bs to As, and don't screw up the As."

That became the mandate. Not to create "training." Not to build a binder full of theory nobody would use. But to create something that worked—repeatable, practical, field-tested, and simple enough that even a guy who just got dragged around by his tie could use it.

Building the First Playbook

So we got to work. No fancy consultants. No glossy PowerPoints. Just three guys and some flip charts asking: What actually works? What do the top reps do differently? How do we make it simple enough that people will use it daily?

We didn't know it then, but this was the beginning of PRECISE Selling.

We created the first version: the flow of a call, the psychology of resistance, the power of asking questions, the magic of listening, how to prepare, how to present, how to handle objections, how to earn agreement.

And when we trained people on it... something incredible happened.

The Proof It Worked

Before we rolled out the training, our sales numbers were embarrassingly lopsided: 17% of our reps sold 85% of our total revenue. A handful of heroes and a whole lot of spectators.

Six months after training everyone on the new methodology, 70% of our reps were selling 85% of our product.

Same company. Same territories. Same products. The only thing we changed was how they communicated, prepared, questioned, listened, presented, earned trust, and closed.

That's when I realized something undeniable:

Salespeople aren't born. They're built.

And they're built through repetition.

You don't rise to the level of your potential.

You fall to the level of your preparation.

The System of Transformation

That day I realized the greatest product I would ever sell was not a medical device. It was a sales system that transforms careers.

Products come and go. Companies get acquired. Territories change.

But sales skill? That's forever.

I started traveling with reps every week—running boot camps, then jumping in the field to coach side-by-side. The ones who embraced the methodology started winning. Small wins at first. But consistently. Predictably. Repeatably.

Soon the wins got bigger. Confidence rose. Numbers rose. Posture changed. Income changed. Lives changed.

That's when I knew: this wasn't "training."

It was a system of transformation.

Your 20-Day Challenge

Now this is where you come in.

This book is not a memoir. It's a manual. The same system that started in that hotel meeting room is the system you're holding in your hands right now.

This book is a blueprint used by top field reps, cold callers making hundreds of calls a day, SDR teams across industries, closers presenting six-figure deals, and entire companies who want repeatable revenue. You're not reading something I used to teach. You're reading what I still teach today.

Give me 20 days. Follow the process. Do the work.

And you'll never sell the same way again.

Why Sprinting Works (And Your Brain Will Resist)

Change doesn't happen because you "ease into it." Real change happens when you sprint.

Sales reps who "ease into" a new system never see results. They dabble. They half-commit. They test the water with a toe when the only thing that works is a cannonball off the high dive.

The human brain is designed to protect you from effort, embarrassment, and discomfort. That's great for survival. Terrible for selling.

Most salespeople plateau because they stop learning long before they stop selling. Their calendars stay full, but their skills stay flat.

During this process, your brain will give you excuses—"This feels awkward," "This isn't my style," "I don't want to sound scripted," "I'll try it after my busy week"—but these are sabotage scripts, not thoughtful insights.

Here's the mind-bender: your brain will prefer failing the old way over winning the new way because failing the old way feels familiar.

Comfort is the real enemy.

For the next 20 days, do not trust your feelings. Trust the process.

Your feelings lie.

The process doesn't.

You don't rise to your motivation.

You rise to your methodology.

How to Read This Book

Read one chapter per day—no skipping.

Do the exercises. Practice out loud, not in your head. Share what you're learning with someone. Accountability multiplies results.

Your First Blind Spot

Before we dive into the PRECISE Playbook—before posture, swagger, objections, or presentations—you need to understand why everything you've been doing has felt harder than it should.

Most salespeople—new ones, veterans, top reps, bottom reps—ALL make one fatal mistake:

They talk too damn much.

Not because they're arrogant.

Not because they don't care.

They talk too much because they think it proves value, they're afraid of silence, they confuse enthusiasm with effectiveness, and nobody ever taught them the science behind communication.

I didn't know any of this until I got dragged down a hallway by a man who examines butts for a living.

That's when I learned the most important law in all of selling:

The more you talk, the more resistance you create.

The more resistance you create, the harder the sale becomes.

This is not opinion. This is physics. Comfort psychology. Human nature.

Your entire sales career will feel twice as hard and produce half the results until you understand the trap your own mouth sets for you.

That's where Chapter 2 begins—not with scripts, not with posture, but with the thing that sabotages more sales than anything else:

Your need to talk.

Let's fix that.

Day 1 begins now.

Why You Lose When You Talk Too Much

The Science of Resistance and the Trap Every Salesperson Falls Into

You're not going to like this chapter.

At least not at first.

Because this is where I tell you something that feels personal, uncomfortable, and just a little bit insulting:

You talk too much.

Not because you're arrogant.

Not because you're a bad person.

Not because you're inexperienced.

You talk too much because you're a salesperson.

And talking feels natural.

When you talk, you feel smart.

You feel in control.

You feel like you're creating value, teaching, moving the sale forward.

But here's the problem:

The more YOU talk, the more THEY resist.

And I don t mean resist like "They're thinking about it."

I mean resist like:

walls go up

trust goes down

skepticism rises

interest collapses

and internally, the buyer is screaming "Please stop talking."

You prescribe before you diagnose. And buyers feel it.

Every salesperson on earth struggles with this. Brand new reps struggle with it. Veteran reps struggle with it. Even top performers fall into the trap.

Because talking feels like selling.

But talking is what's quietly destroying your sales.

The Universal Law of Buyer Behavior

Human beings are wired to push back against force. It's not a personality trait—it's a survival instinct. If something pushes on you, you push back.

Every statement you make as a salesperson triggers a tiny defensive reaction:

Is this true? Do I believe this? Do I trust this? Is this biased? Are they exaggerating? What's the angle?

That internal questioning is resistance in motion.

And the louder or longer you talk, the louder that inner resistance grows.

Great sales isn't about delivering information. It's about lowering resistance.

But talking raises it. Fast.

Why Salespeople Talk Too Much

Let's call out the real reasons. Not the polite ones—the real ones.

Silence feels terrifying. Most reps equate silence with failure, so they fill the air with sound. The irony is that silence is one of the most professional signals you can send.

Talking feels safer than asking. Questions feel risky. Talking feels like control. They're afraid the buyer will ask something they can't answer, so they build a giant wall of words to protect themselves.

Habit. They learned from other talkers. The industry is full of "pitchers," not professionals.

Insecurity. Nothing hides fear like over-explaining.

Lack of preparation. When you don't have a plan, you talk. When you don't know what questions to ask, you talk. When your brain panics, you talk. Talking becomes a survival mechanism—but it's the very thing killing your deals.

If you manage a team, you already see this: the reps who talk the most in meetings usually struggle the most in front of customers.

The Hidden Cost of Too Many Statements

Every statement you make carries an emotional price tag. To you, it feels like value. To them, it feels like pressure.

You say: "Our customers love this feature."

They think: "Everyone says that."

You say: "This will save you time."

They think: "Prove it."

You say: "You're going to love this."

They think: "I'll decide that."

You say: "You'll see ROI in 90 days."

They think: "What happens on day 91?"

It's not that your statements are wrong. It's that the buyer's brain is built to defend against them. Every statement creates a micro-objection in their head—not because you're wrong, but because that's how brains work when someone is talking at them.

Statements feel risky. Questions feel safe. And humans follow the path of least risk.

Talking Less Doesn't Mean Losing Control

This is where reps get nervous. They hear "talk less" and think: "So I'm just supposed to sit there like a mute monk and hope for the best?"

No.

It means taking control in a different way.

Amateurs think control comes from talking. Pros know control comes from the questions they choose, the order they ask them in, and what they do with the answers. They still drive the conversation—they just use a steering wheel instead of a megaphone.

The Reel-In Effect

Sales isn't hunting. It's fishing.

You don't rip the rod when a fish bites. You tug—just enough to get movement.

Questions are tugs. Statements are violent jerks.

The best salespeople guide the buyer gently: one question, one insight, one pause, one acknowledgment, one step at a time. They don't pull the buyer toward the finish line. They let the buyer walk there on their own.

Talking is force.

Questions are gravity.

Gravity wins.

The "Shut Up Threshold"

Every buyer has an internal threshold for how long they'll let you talk before they mentally check out.

It's short. Seven seconds. Maybe ten if they like you. Fifteen if you're charming. Twenty if you're a unicorn.

After that, you're just noise.

The minute you cross their shut-up threshold, their brain goes into polite survival mode. They smile. They nod. They act interested. They give short answers. Then they ghost you.

Not because you didn't have a good product—but because you never gave them a chance to participate in the sale.

People don't buy what they hear. They buy what they say.

And when you talk too much, they say nothing. Which means they buy nothing.

The Illusion of a Good Call

Every rep has had this experience:

You walk out of a call thinking, "That was great! They loved me!"

Then the buyer ghosts. Or goes silent. Or delays. Or "re-evaluates priorities." Or drifts into the abyss of "no update yet."

Why?

Because the call only felt great to you. You did all the talking. You felt in flow, smart, powerful, like you crushed it.

Meanwhile, the buyer felt overwhelmed, passive, unseen, unheard, pressured—like they were sitting in a lecture they didn't sign up for.

Talking makes the call feel great for the seller and terrible for the buyer.

Buyers Aren't Rational First—They're Emotional First

Buyers rarely reject you because of facts. They reject you because of feelings: "I feel overwhelmed. I feel pressured. I feel uncertain. I feel like they don't get it. I feel talked at, not talked with."

Sales is emotional long before it becomes logical.

Talking appeals to logic. Questions appeal to emotion.

Talking tells. Questions invite.

Talking pushes. Questions open.

And buyers follow open doors, not closed ones.

The Buyer's Secret Desire

Buyers don't want a perfect product, a perfect pitch, a perfect rep, or a perfect presentation.

They want one thing: a moment of clarity.

When someone talks too much, clarity disappears. When someone asks the right question, clarity appears.

The right question can do more in three seconds than a pitch can do in thirty minutes. Because clarity feels like relief.

"Oh, that's what's bothering me."

"Oh, that's the real problem."

"Oh, THAT'S what I want."

Talking creates fog. Questions create clarity.

Your job isn't to flood the buyer. Your job is to reveal the truth.

Where the PRECISE Playbook Comes In

This is exactly why the PRECISE Playbook exists.

Every move you'll learn in the coming chapters—Prepare, Respect, Engage, Convey, Indecision, Secure, Explore—is built to keep you out of the talking trap and force you to sell like a pro: asking first, listening hard, then making short, sharp statements instead of firing off your memory pitch.

The Shift That Changes Everything

Remember the proctologist from Chapter 1?

"You're supposed to diagnose before you prescribe. You did the opposite."

That's the shift.

You're no longer a presenter. You're a discoverer.

And discoverers diagnose before they prescribe.

Presenters talk. Discoverers ask.

Presenters teach. Discoverers reveal.

Presenters perform. Discoverers guide.

Presenters chase. Discoverers attract.

This book is going to turn you from a presenter into a discoverer.

And it starts in the next chapter.

Because now that you understand why talking destroys your sales, it's time to learn the opposite: the art of asking the right questions.

That's where the sale begins.

That's where the buyer opens up.

That's where the resistance disappears.

That's where the truth comes out.

That's where trust forms.

That's where the magic happens.

If you never changed anything else in your selling except this—talk less, ask more, listen deeper—you'd still see a dramatic lift in your pipeline and close rates.

Day 2 begins now.

CHAPTER 3

Why the Pros Ask More Questions Than They Answer

By now you've accepted a painful but liberating truth: you talk too much.

Welcome to the club.

But the pros eventually discover a superpower that changes everything:

Questions close deals. Statements kill deals.

Statements create resistance. Questions melt it.

The difference between a top 1% seller and a middle-of-the-pack talker is not product knowledge, charisma, extroversion, or some mythical "sales gene."

It's this: pros ask more questions than they answer—because they understand exactly what questions do.

Most reps think they ask questions. They don't. They ask a few predictable, surface-level things like "How many employees do you have?" or "What's your timeline?" Those are fine—but they aren't the questions that change the sale.

Great sellers use questions strategically, psychologically, and intentionally.

And there are nine very real reasons they do it.

But first, let's talk about how you got here.

The Talker's Delusion

Most reps grew up in a world where being quick, witty, charming, or charismatic earned them rewards. You got laughs. You got attention.

You got praise. You got job offers. You got away with not studying. You got dates.

Then that same social skillset became your early sales identity.

People told you:

"You're a natural."

"You should be in sales."

"You're such a good talker."

Nobody realized how destructive that sentence would be for your career.

Because what works socially does not work in sales.

In sales, the talker loses. The explainer loses. The rambler loses. The presenter loses. The human product brochure loses.

Do you know who wins?

The rep who asks the right questions and listens like they actually care.

Pitch Bot 3000: The Salesperson You Don't Want to Be

Let me introduce you to an old friend: Pitch Bot 3000.

Pitch Bot has the personality of a fax machine and the self-awareness of a traffic cone.

Pitch Bot does three things well: talks, talks, and talks loudly.

Pitch Bot never asks a question. Pitch Bot doesn't need to know what you want. Pitch Bot doesn't care about your pain points. Pitch Bot has a script from 1987 and he's gonna use it, dammit.

Pitch Bot is the rep who enters every meeting with a 30-slide deck, opens his laptop before saying hello, starts pitching before the buyer sits down, thinks listening is optional, over-explains everything, and treats questions as speed bumps.

Every company has at least one Pitch Bot.

And every rep reading this has been a Pitch Bot at some point. Yes, even you. Especially you.

If you've ever said something like "I don't need a process—I know how to read people" or "I just let the conversation flow naturally" or "I like to feel it out on the fly"—you've had a little Pitch Bot in you.

The good news? There's a cure. A simple one.

Ask more questions. Better questions. Smarter questions. Earlier questions. Consistent questions.

You've Been Rewarded for Talking, Not for Asking

From childhood into your twenties, all your feedback loops reinforced talking. Class participation? Talking. College discussions? Talking. Interviews? Talking. First dates? Definitely talking.

But almost no one said: "That was an exquisite question" or "The way you got them to open up was brilliant."

No one becomes a top salesperson "naturally." It's learned. It's practiced. It's coached.

Ask my SDRs. Every one of them walks in believing they're good talkers. In the first week, I break them of that fantasy. Because talking without curiosity is noise. And noise doesn't book meetings, build trust, uncover pain, create urgency, or close deals.

Sales is not noise. Sales is discovery.

The Nine Reasons Pros Ask Questions

Here's why great sellers rely on questions—and how you can start doing the same.

1. Questions tell you what the buyer actually wants. Most reps pitch what they think the buyer should care about. Pros dig until they uncover what actually triggered the meeting.

Great question: "Walk me through what pushed this initiative to the top of your priority list."

That question uncovers the frustration, the politics, the trigger event, the consequences, and the emotional charge behind the change. Deals begin with truth, not assumption.

SDR version: "What made you take this call today instead of deleting my email like a normal person?"

Closer version: "What's the internal pain that finally made this urgent?"

2. Questions reduce resistance. Statements raise defenses. Questions lower them. When you state things, the buyer subconsciously thinks: "Is that true? Is he overselling me? What's the catch?" When you ask, their guard drops because they become the one doing the talking.

Great question: "Before we go too far—what matters most to you in a solution like this?"

SDR version: "Where do things break down most today?"

Closer version: "When you evaluate different options, what criteria do you personally care about most?"

Questions open the door. Statements slam it.

3. Questions create emotional safety. People tell the truth when they feel safe—not when they feel sold. You create emotional safety by showing humility.

Great question: "I might be wrong—help me understand your biggest frustration with this right now."

SDR version: "What's the toughest part of this for you day-to-day?"

Closer version: "Who feels this problem the most inside your org?"

Buyers reveal what's real when they feel protected.

4. Questions give you control while the buyer feels in control. This is psychological jiu-jitsu. When you ask the right questions, you steer the meeting—while the buyer feels like they're steering.

Great question: "What's the best place for us to start?"

SDR version: "Where should we focus first?"

Closer version: "Who besides you needs to weigh in on this?"

You're driving the car. They think they're picking the music.

If you manage a team, you already see this: when a rep finally chooses a question instead of a monologue, the whole room relaxes.

5. Buyers trust their own voice more than yours. A buyer will always believe what they say more than what you say. Your statements feel salesy. Their statements feel like conviction.

Instead of telling them "This is costing you time," ask: "What happens if this stays the same through next quarter?"

Let them sell urgency out loud.

I watched an SDR transform a skeptical prospect using this exact principle. The prospect said: "We're probably fine waiting until next year."

The SDR could have argued: "But you're losing money every day!" Instead, he asked: "Walk me through what happens between now and next year if nothing changes."

Silence.

Then the prospect said: "Well... we keep losing those hours. And my team keeps complaining. And honestly, by next year we'll probably have lost another person because of this frustration."

The SDR didn't have to say another word. The prospect talked himself into urgency.

Your pitch doesn't move deals. Their realization does.

6. Questions prepare the buyer to sell internally. Every buyer becomes your salesperson in the meeting you will NOT attend: the CFO meeting, the internal committee, the leadership huddle. Questions help them rehearse your message out loud.

Great question: "If your VP asks why you're considering this, what will you tell them?"

SDR version: "Who internally will care the most about this?"

Closer version: "What does your CFO need to hear for this to move forward?"

That forces them to practice your pitch—without you ever giving them a script.

But there's a process underneath that principle—one I teach in every seminar. I call it the Next Level Process. Here's how it works.

Step 1: Try to get in the meeting. This is where every sale starts. You're prospecting, working to earn the first conversation.

Step 2: Get the Big Fat Yes from the person in front of you. Run PRECISE. Prepare, earn respect, engage with questions, convey your solution, handle indecision, and secure agreement. Get the person sitting across from you to say yes—enthusiastically.

Step 3: "Who else is involved?" Once they're bought in, find out who else needs to weigh in. There's almost always someone.

Step 4: Try to get in the meeting...with the Big Wig. This is the move most reps skip—and it's the most important one. Don't assume you need to send your champion in alone. Ask directly: "Joe, would it be helpful for you for me to make myself available for that meeting, should any questions come up regarding our solution?" That's not pushy. That's professional. You're offering to make their job easier. Most of the time, they'll say yes—and now you're in the room where the decision gets made.

If they say yes, you're in. Prepare for that meeting and run PRECISE again with the decision-maker. But if they say, "Let me handle it first"—and sometimes they will—you don't panic. You shift to the Next Level Prep:

Step 5: "What are they going to need to hear or know to help them come to the same conclusion you did?" This is the question that turns your buyer into your salesperson. You're asking them to rehearse the internal pitch—out loud, in front of you—so you can coach it in real time. If they stumble, you know exactly where the message needs tightening.

Step 6: Provide specific info and materials. Now you arm them. Not with your forty-page deck—with the two or three pieces that address exactly what the decision-maker cares about. You know what those are because your buyer just told you in Step 5.

Six steps. Always try to get in the room first. If you can't, prep your champion so well that it's almost like you're there. That's the power of asking questions that prepare them to sell internally.

7. Questions create micro-yeses. No deal is closed with one yes. Deals are closed with a series of small agreements.

Great question: "So that's accurate—you're losing a few hours a week because of this?"

Buyer: "Yes."

Micro-yes. Each small yes is a shove on the flywheel.

8. Questions isolate concerns early. Objections don't magically show up at the end. They grow quietly while you talk too much. If you ask early, you can defuse them early.

Great question: "Before we go deeper—what concerns or hesitations pop into your mind right away?"

SDR version: "What would make this a no?"

Closer version: "What would stop this internally?"

Objections are easiest to fix when they're tiny—not when the buyer has already slid into ghost mode.

9. Questions shift you from performer to guide. Performers talk to impress. Guides ask to understand. Performers rely on charisma. Guides rely on curiosity. Performers pitch. Guides diagnose.

Great question: "Before I show anything—what does success look like for you?"

SDR version: "What's the goal on your side?"

Closer version: "What outcome tells you this was the right move?"

Guides win more often than performers. Every time.

The Three-Question Rule

Here's a simple test to know if you're asking enough questions:

For every statement you make, you should ask at least three questions first.

Most reps do the opposite: three statements, one question. That's backwards.

Here's what 3:1 looks like in practice:

Bad (1 question, 3 statements):

Rep: "How many locations do you have?"

Buyer: "Five."

Rep: "Great! We work with companies your size all the time. Our solution is really easy to implement. And we can get you up and running in 30 days."

The buyer's guard just went up.

Good (3 questions, 1 statement):

Rep: "How many locations do you have?"

Buyer: "Five."

Rep: "Got it. Which of those five locations feels this problem the most?"

Buyer: "Probably our main office and the newer site."

Rep: "What makes those two different from the others?"

Buyer: "Well, those are the ones with newer teams, so the onboarding pain is worse there."

Rep: "That makes sense—newer teams, more onboarding friction."

See the difference?

The bad version talked AT the buyer. The good version uncovered specific pain.

Your assignment: hit 3:1 on your next 10 calls. Track it. You'll be shocked how hard it is at first—and how powerful it becomes once you nail it.

The Thinking-On-Your-Feet Exercise

At every PRECISE bootcamp, I run the same exercise. And every single time—every single group—the room falls apart laughing.

Not because the exercise is funny at first... but because it reveals exactly how bad people are at showing curiosity.

Here's how I set it up:

"Turn to the person next to you. One of you is Person A. One is Person B. Person A—make a statement about yourself. Anything. Then ask Person B a question. Person B—answer the question... and then ask a NEW question back."

Simple, right?

Wrong.

Every time, this happens:

Person A nails it. They say something like: "I love playing golf" or "I'm addicted to pickleball" or "I've binged every episode of Yellowstone twice."

Then they follow with a question: "What do you like to do?"

Perfect.

Then Person B answers—and their brain completely melts.

They say something like: "Oh, I love skiing... and cooking... and being with my family."

And then they freeze. They look around, confused. Looking for help. Wondering what they're supposed to do next.

That silence? That confused look? That awkward moment?

That is exactly why they struggle in sales.

Because Person B—like most salespeople—has spent their entire life answering questions... not asking them.

They don't know how to keep curiosity going. They don't know how to draw someone out. They don't know how to explore.

And you cannot win in sales without exploration.

This exercise hits people so hard because they realize: they have been trained to talk. They have not been trained to care.

And caring—real curiosity—is what makes you great.

The SDR Who Went From 2 Meetings to 12

One of my SDRs—let's call her Sarah—was stuck at 2–3 meetings per week for months.

She worked hard. She made 400 calls a week. She followed the script.

But she talked too much.

I listened to her calls and heard the same pattern:

Prospect: "We're pretty happy with our current setup."

Sarah: "Well, let me tell you why we're different. We have better reporting, faster implementation, and dedicated support..." (monologue for 45 seconds)

Prospect: click

So I gave her one rule: ask three questions before making any statement.

She hated it at first. It felt unnatural. It felt slow.

But within two weeks? Twelve meetings in one week.

Why?

Because instead of talking through objections, she started asking through them:

Prospect: "We're pretty happy with our current setup."

Sarah: "Got it. What does 'pretty happy' mean—like you'd give it an 8 out of 10, or more like a 6?"

Prospect: "Honestly? Maybe a 6."

Sarah: "What would it take to make it an 8?"

Prospect: "Well, the reporting is kind of a pain..."

And the door opened.

Questions didn't just help her book more meetings—they helped her book BETTER meetings. Because when prospects talk themselves into the problem, they show up to the meeting already half-sold.

What Questions Actually Do

Now let me tell you the deeper truth:

Questions aren't just a sales technique. They are a human technique.

People are starving for someone who actually listens.

Your buyers live in a world where nobody listens at home, nobody listens at work, nobody listens in meetings, nobody listens on calls. Everyone is rushing. Everyone is interrupting. Everyone is pitching. Everyone is performing.

When you ask real questions—thoughtful, curious, human questions—you instantly become different.

Not because you're a great salesperson... but because you're a great listener.

Buyers open up. Walls drop. Trust forms. Urgency builds. Truth comes out. Deals accelerate.

Questions aren't what you do.

Questions are who you become.

Where the PRECISE Playbook Comes In

Now that you understand why questions work, you might be wondering: "Okay, Sully. I get it. Questions are powerful. But WHAT questions should I actually ask?"

That's where the CLEAR framework comes in—and that's what the next chapter will teach you.

CLEAR gives you the exact questions to ask, in the exact order, to uncover truth and build trust without sounding like an interrogator. It's the questioning system inside the PRECISE Playbook.

But before we get there, internalize one final truth:

Questioning isn't a technique you add to your toolkit.

It's a mindset that replaces everything else.

Day 3 begins now.

CHAPTER 4

Listen Up... To Learn

Exposing Fake Listening in Sales

Let's start this chapter with a confession:

Most people don't know how to listen.

Most salespeople REALLY don't know how to listen.

And if you're married, divorced, have kids, have ever worked with other humans, or have ever sat through a meeting where someone said "circle back," you already know this.

Listening is the most overestimated, overclaimed, and underdeveloped skill in the sales profession.

Ask any room of salespeople: "Who here considers themselves a good listener?"

Every hand shoots up like they're getting graded.

Ask: "Who here considers themselves a fake listener?"

Maybe four hands rise slowly—the honest ones.

Then I ask the real question: "If you're married, divorced, or have children, please raise your hand."

And suddenly the room looks like a Beyoncé concert.

Because deep down, everyone knows the truth:

Humans are world-class fake listeners.

Salespeople are Olympic-level fake listeners.

And yet nothing—absolutely nothing—will determine your success in sales more than your ability to truly listen.

Not "uh-huh, uh-huh, got it." Not "I hear you." Not "I was listening with my eyes."

I'm talking about real, active, curious, attentive listening. The kind where the other person feels understood. The kind where the conversation slows down. The kind where the buyer starts saying things they haven't said to anyone else.

But most reps never get to that level because they're too busy doing what fake listeners do: rehearsing what they're going to say next, waiting for the buyer to stop talking, nodding politely while mentally returning a text message, "listening" only for the parts that match their pitch.

And the hilarious part? They think they're fooling everybody.

You're not.

Buyers know when you're fake listening. Your spouse knows. Your kids know. Your dog knows. You're not subtle.

You Don't Know You're Fake Listening Because Fake Listening Feels Like Listening

Here's the sneaky part: fake listening feels like real listening to the person doing it.

But here's how you know you're faking it: You can repeat their words, but you can't explain their meaning. You nod at the right times, but your mind is five miles away. You hear the sound, but not the substance. You're present physically, but not mentally.

You know how many sales reps I've coached who told me "I think I'm a good listener"? About 100% of them.

You know how many actually were? About 7%.

The other 93% were using what I call competitive listening—the fake skill where you pretend to listen but you're actually just waiting to win the conversation.

Competitive listening looks like: interrupting with excitement, finishing their sentences incorrectly, solving a problem before they finish describing it, correcting them mid-thought, talking over them, filling silence the moment it appears, looking for the angle instead of the truth.

Competitive listening kills trust.

Real listening builds it.

Most Reps Don't Listen Because Listening Requires Slowing Down

One of the biggest reasons reps don't listen well is simple: listening requires slowing down. And most salespeople live their entire careers in fast-forward mode.

They're thinking: "What's my next question? Where is this going? What's the perfect response? How do I get them to yes? How do I sound smart right now?"

Listening requires you to stop strategizing and start understanding. But understanding takes patience. Patience takes discipline. Discipline takes awareness. Awareness takes maturity.

Listening is a mental workout, not a resting state.

You have to fight your natural urge to interrupt, fix, defend, jump in, pitch, rescue, explain, and speed things up.

Most reps refuse to fight that urge.

Top reps win because they do.

Listening Isn't Passive—It's a Competitive Advantage

People assume listening is passive. It isn't. Listening is active— brutally active.

Listening is reading between the lines. Listening is catching what they didn't say. Listening is noting tone, pacing, and hesitation. Listening is diagnosing the issue behind the issue. Listening is identifying fear, pressure, politics, ego, or emotion.

Listening is noticing a contradiction and circling back with one clarifying question that changes the whole call.

Listening is:

"Tell me more about that."

"You paused—what was that about?"

"That sounded stressful—what happened next?"

Listening gets you into rooms that pitch-monkeys can't access.

But let me tell you the real reason listening matters:

Listening makes people feel important.

And people buy from people who make them feel important.

Not from people who make themselves sound important.

The Day I Learned I Was a Fake Listener

Every time I teach listening skills in a bootcamp, I ask: "Okay—who here is a fake listener?"

A few hands go up.

Then I say: "If you're married, divorced, or have kids... please raise your hand."

Now I've got 90% of the room.

Because we all fake listen. We just hate admitting it.

And the hardest truth of all? You can think you're a great listener... You can teach listening... You can write about listening... and still be terrible at it.

And the way I learned that was one of the most embarrassing moments of my life.

Let's go back in time.

The Day I Tried to Write the Worst Chapter Ever Written

This happened right when I decided to write my original book.

I was still under a consulting contract with my former medical company. I had been traveling Monday through Thursday. I had ZERO intention of ever writing a book.

But every time I spoke at industry events, reps would line up afterward and say: "Where can we learn more?"

And I had nothing to give them except a handshake, a smile, and a hollow "Stay in touch!"

So I made myself a promise: 20 weeks. 20 chapters. No weekend fun until the chapter is done.

If you ever want to get something finished, deny yourself alcohol and leisure until the work is done—highly effective.

So it's Thursday. 4:00pm. I'm exhausted.

I sit down to write the Listening Skills chapter—the very thing I teach for a living.

And I start typing. And the words are HORRIBLE. Cringe-inducing. The stuff that makes editors quit the industry.

I'm writing nonsense like: "Be a good listener when people talk to you with words."

Words? As opposed to when they tap Morse code on my forehead?

I mean, this wasn't a chapter—it was a cry for help.

And right as I'm battling through the worst first draft in history...

...the office door flies open.

Enter Jake Sullivan, Four and a Half Years Old, High on Kindergarten & Elmer's Glue

My little boy Jake comes bursting in like Kramer on Seinfeld:

"Daddy! Daddy! Look at this! I made a construction paper apple tree in kindergarten! And I got to use the Elmer's glue! Look! It's still on my hands! But we can only use the round scissors because the sharp ones are dangerous!"

He was giving me a full sales presentation: visual aids, enthusiasm, benefits, features, emotional connection, demonstration, urgency ("glue's still on my hands!"), clear target audience (Dad).

And what was I doing?

The patented Dad Fake-Listening Technique™.

I'm staring at my computer screen, nodding like a bobblehead with a neck injury:

"Oh, Elmer's glue! Oh, round scissors! Oh, kindergarten apple tree! That's great, buddy!"

Not one ounce of presence. Not a drop of sincerity.

I was throwing out keyword callbacks just to keep him believing I was interested.

He kept talking... and I kept typing.

Eventually, my lack of interest leaked out through my body language.

His face dropped.

He turned and started walking away.

And what did I say?

The classic Fake Listener's Benediction:

"Hey buddy, that's really important. I want to see it. Leave it on the kitchen counter. And, uh... shut the door behind you. Love you."

Door closes. Gone. Silence.

8 PM—The Punch in the Gut

Four hours later—around 8:00pm—I finish the chapter.

I read the last line I typed:

"Don't ever fake listen, especially with your most important customers. They will know you're faking—and they won't forgive you."

And it hit me.

I felt something in my stomach—the kind of feeling you get right before a really bad realization.

I stood up. Walked through the house. Burst through the door into the kitchen like a man on a mission.

And there's Jake. My little guy. Happy. Carefree. Still in pajamas with a dinosaur on them.

I say:

"Jakey, Jakey—show me what you made! Where's your apple tree? You made a construction paper apple tree!"

And he says the words that crushed me:

"No, it's okay Daddy."

I said: "No. I want to see it!"

Still: "No... it's okay Daddy."

Finally, he says:

"I showed it to Mommy. She put it in the cabinet where she puts all the things I make for her."

And immediately this wave washed over me—the realization that I wasn't listening to my most important customers.

The people I loved most were getting the worst version of me.

If I couldn't listen to the people I loved most... how was I showing up for my paying customers?

And if it's this easy to fake listen to the people you love most, imagine how easy it is to fake listen to a buyer you met eight minutes ago.

Listening Isn't a Skill—It's a Respect Issue

Buyers don't forgive fake listening. Kids don't either.

Because fake listening says: "You're not important enough for my full attention."

Real listening says: "You matter. Your words matter. Your feelings matter. Your world matters. I care."

Here's the truth I realized that night:

Listening isn't about technique.

Listening is about respect.

People can feel when you're with them. They can feel when you're not.

If you can't respect the people you love enough to listen, you won't magically respect a stranger on a Tuesday demo.

Buyers remember the reps who truly listen.

Kids remember the parents who don't.

The 5-Channel Listener

If questioning is the engine of great selling... listening is the transmission.

Questions don't matter if you don't listen to the answers.

Most reps don't listen. They wait to talk. They aren't receiving information. They're loading their next statement like a crossbow.

Pros don't do that. Pros listen like detectives. Pros listen like comedians reading a room.

And the highest-level pros—the ones smashing quota and getting callbacks the same afternoon—they listen like this:

1. Listen with your ears. This is the baseline. But even here, most reps fail because they're multitasking—clicking around their CRM, checking Slack, toggling between windows. Technology has made fake listening easier than ever. Elite reps listen without distraction. They stay in the moment. They ask follow-ups based on the last three words the buyer said—not the last three bullet points in their slide deck.

Simple test: If the buyer says something important and you don't ask a follow-up question... you weren't listening. You were waiting.

2. Listen with your eyes. Watching is listening. Great listeners don't just hear the words. They notice the micro-winces, the eyebrow dips, the long blinks, the shoulder drops, the inhale before answering, the glance to the side.

Even on Zoom, you can see everything you need to: If you ask a pricing question and they shift in their chair? That's a concern. If you mention implementation and they lean back? That's fear. Eyes tell the truth long before words do.

3. Listen with your body. Pros match energy. They don't bulldoze it. When a buyer is quiet and introspective—pros don't turn into game show hosts. When a buyer is excited—pros reflect the enthusiasm. When a buyer is nervous—pros become calm.

I was on a call with a VP who was explaining their current process. His energy was flat, monotone, almost defeated. A typical rep would have jumped in with excitement: "Great! Let me show you how we can fix that!"

But I matched his energy. I slowed down. I spoke quieter. I said:

"That sounds exhausting. How long have you been dealing with this?"

And he exhaled—like he'd been waiting for someone to just acknowledge the weight of it.

"Three years," he said. "And I'm tired of fighting it."

That's when the real conversation started. If I'd bulldozed him with enthusiasm, he would have shut down.

4. Listen with your intuition. This is where reps become dangerous (in a good way). Because great sellers hear things like:

"We're evaluating a few options right now..." which actually means: "We're stuck. Make this easy."

"Budget is... complicated..." which means: "Someone doesn't want to fight this battle internally."

"We just need to think about it..." which means: "You didn't ask the real questions yet."

A buyer's first answer is rarely the real answer. Their second answer is closer. Their third answer—after a great follow-up—is almost always the truth.

5. Listen for what's missing. The unsaid is the gold. If a buyer never mentions internal politics? It matters. If they never talk about urgency? It matters. If they say "we've tried this before" but never explain why it failed? It matters.

The best closers I've ever seen don't just listen to answers... they listen for blanks. They listen for the gap in the story. That's where the deal lives.

The Final Listening Test

If you want to know—REALLY know—whether you're a great listener or not... here's the test:

After your next call, answer this question: "Could I repeat, with accuracy, what the buyer said, why they said it, what mattered most to them, and what they were worried about?"

If the answer is no? You weren't listening. You were performing.

Performers lose.

Guides win.

And great guides listen like their paycheck depends on it—because it does.

Where the PRECISE Playbook Comes In

Listening isn't a separate step in the PRECISE Playbook—it's the foundation underneath every move.

Without listening, you can't prepare properly. Without listening, you can't build respect or trust. Without listening, your questions fall flat. Without listening, you can't tailor your message. Without listening, you can't handle objections. Without listening, you can't secure commitment.

Every move in PRECISE depends on your ability to truly listen.

Without it, you're just running a script. And scripts don't close deals. Relationships do.

Your Assignment: Day 4

Here's your challenge for Day 4:

Home test: Ask one "number one customer" (spouse, partner, kid, best friend): "Am I a good listener?" Then shut up and listen to the answer. Don't defend. Don't explain. Don't justify. Just listen.

Call test: On your next recorded call, re-listen with one goal: write down everything the buyer said about their world—not what you said.

Let silence do the heavy lifting. Let curiosity and respect drive the conversation.

This is where trust is built. This is where deals come alive. This is where your career starts to transform.

As I always tell my reps—all of them hammering hundreds of calls a day:

"If you can't listen to your number one customers, you'll never listen to your number two customers And the number twos? They're the ones signing checks."

Day 4 begins now.

PART II

THREE ELEMENTS OF THE
PRECISE PLAYBOOK

PRECISE Selling Playbook

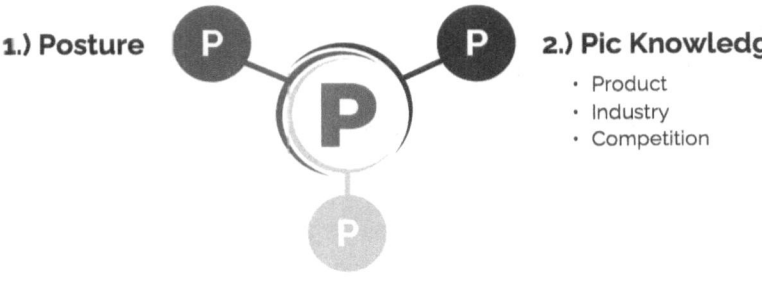

1.) Posture

2.) Pic Knowledge
- Product
- Industry
- Competition

3.) PRECISE Actions

CHAPTER 5

Posture

The Spirit Behind Every Sale

If you've made it this far in the book, you've survived the part where we talk about asking great questions and actually listening to human beings. That alone puts you in the top 10% of salespeople.

But now we need to talk about something most reps underestimate, ignore, or flat-out sleepwalk through:

Posture.

Most people think sales training is all about the steps. The process. The objections. The techniques. The framework. (And yes—that's coming.)

But here's the truth:

You can follow every step perfectly... but if your posture stinks? You lose.

Posture is the spirit of the salesperson. The energy. The attitude. The playfulness. The confidence. The creativity. The humanity.

It's the part buyers feel the moment you show up—before you ask a question, before you show a product, before you even say hello.

Posture is the spark.

And most reps treat it like a cigarette butt they flick out the window.

Posture: Boring vs. Brilliant

Let's start with a painful truth: Most salespeople are boring.

Boring posture. Boring intros. Boring emails. Boring calls. Boring follow-up. Boring visits.

They show up with the same energy as a DMV line. Their emails read like a warranty pamphlet. Their calls sound like they're awake but resent it.

Then they wonder: "Why don't buyers call me back?"

Because nothing about them creates a feeling. Nothing about them makes people say: "I like this rep." Nothing stands out.

Posture—the creative, fun, human side of selling—is the missing ingredient. It's the difference between a buyer thinking "Ugh, here we go..." versus "Okay... I'll give this person a shot."

Why Posture Beats Talent

I've seen reps with average product knowledge, average questioning skills, and average experience CRUSH reps with more talent for one reason: Their posture was elite.

Why? Because buyers don't decide based on who is the smartest. They decide based on who makes them feel comfortable, who makes them smile, who brings positive energy, who treats them like a human, who surprises them, who is memorable.

Posture is where all of that begins.

The Day I Learned Posture Matters More Than Product Knowledge

Early in my Welch Allyn days, I was struggling.

I knew my products cold. I could recite specs in my sleep. I had the features, benefits, and competitive advantages memorized.

But I wasn't winning.

One day, I'm walking through a hospital hallway—dejected, frustrated, ready to quit—when I see another rep. Not from my company. Not even in my industry.

He sold hospital furniture. Chairs.

And the nurses were SWARMING him.

Laughing. High-fiving. Asking when he'd be back.

I watched. He wasn't pitching. He wasn't selling. He was present. Energized. Joyful. Curious. Fun.

He remembered names. He asked about kids. He brought coffee. He made people feel good.

And I realized something that changed my entire career:

People don't buy from the smartest rep.

They buy from the rep who makes them feel something.

I went home that night and made a decision: From now on, I would walk into every room like I was entering a party—not a transaction. I would bring energy, humor, warmth, and humanity. I would stop trying to be the most knowledgeable rep and start trying to be the most memorable one.

And everything changed. Buyers started calling me back. Referrals started showing up. Deals started closing.

Not because I got smarter. Because I got human.

That's posture.

Posture Throughout the Conversation

A lot of reps think posture is just how you open. Big smile, strong handshake, decent joke—done.

Wrong.

Posture is an attitude you carry through the entire interaction: when the buyer challenges you, when they say "We tried this before and it didn't work," when they ghost you for three weeks and finally resurface.

An amateur loses posture the moment things get uncomfortable. Their voice tightens. They talk faster. They start overexplaining.

A pro keeps posture when they don't know the answer and calmly say, "Great question—let me check and get you a clean answer by tomorrow." When the buyer says "Your price is high" and they reply, "Totally fair reaction. Can we talk about what you're comparing it to?" When a meeting goes sideways and they still end the call with warmth and a clear next step.

Posture is steady.

It doesn't spike when things are going well and disappear when they're not.

Posture on Bad Days

Posture also shows up on the days you don't feel like selling. You know those days: three no-shows in a row, a deal you were sure about goes dark, your manager pings you with "quick questions" that aren't quick.

On those days, you have a choice.

You can bring your frustration into the next call. The buyer hears it, feels it, and wants to get off the phone.

Or you can decide: "My buyers don't deserve my bad day."

World-class reps learn how to reset their posture between calls: walk, breathe, laugh at something stupid, put on a song, say one sentence out loud that reminds them who they are.

Posture isn't pretending life is perfect.

It's choosing not to dump your emotional garbage on the next human you talk to.

Why We Use the Word "Stupid"

Before we go any further, let's clear something up.

In this book, stupid never means reckless or disrespectful.

Years ago, I noticed something: every negative, grumpy, risk-averse salesperson—the ones in the back with their arms crossed—would watch a competitor do something bold and say: "That's a stupid idea."

Dress up as a nerdy proctologist? "That's stupid." Bake a cake with your phone number in frosting? "Who would do that? Stupid." Use a funny image in an email? "Oh great, another stupid rep trying too hard."

But the salespeople with the MOST "stupid" ideas... had the MOST stupid commission checks. The ones taking risks, having fun, and standing out were the ones winning business and building relationships, while the critics complained their pipeline was dry and their territory was "different."

So I kept the word. I embraced it. And I made it a philosophy.

In PRECISE Selling, stupid means bold, human, creative, unforgettable.

And most importantly... stupid works.

Why Most Reps Never Get Stupid

Here's the real reason most reps stay boring: Fear.

Not fear of failure. Fear of looking foolish.

They'd rather be forgettable than risk being laughed at. They'd rather send the same email 47 other reps sent this week than try something that might get a weird look from their manager.

But here's what they don't understand: Buyers are bored out of their minds.

Every email looks the same. Every voicemail sounds the same. Every Zoom intro follows the same script.

When you do something stupid—something bold, creative, human—you're not being unprofessional. You're being a relief. A break from the monotony. A moment of humanity in a sea of corporate robots.

Buyers don't forward boring emails to their team. They forward the stupid ones.

And forwarding = talking about you = thinking about you = remembering you.

That's how deals start.

The Four Levels of Stupidity

Everything in posture falls into one of four Stupidity Levels.

Stupid is good here. Stupid is memorable. Stupid is lovable. Stupid is irresistible.

Levels 1 and 2 are the things most reps could do but don't. Levels 3 and 4 are the things that take guts—and build legends.

LEVEL 1 — Mildly Stupid

Harmless, low-risk touches that prove you're not a corporate robot. Handwritten thank-you notes. Fun images in emails. Quick memes or GIFs. "Saw this and thought of you" moments.

Level 1 is easy—and almost nobody does it because most reps are "too busy." They tell themselves "I'll do that when I have more time," forgetting that three thoughtful minutes can be worth more than thirty more bland emails.

Example: The Handwritten 'You Were Right' Note. A buyer pushed back on a recommendation during a call. The rep thought about it overnight and realized the buyer was correct. Next morning, a handwritten note arrived: "You were right. I was wrong. Thanks for keeping me honest. Let's talk next week." The buyer called within an hour: "Nobody ever admits they're wrong. I like you."

That's Level 1: low risk, high humanity.

LEVEL 2 — Moderately Stupid

These moves take a little courage and deliver big results.

Creative voicemail greetings. Pattern-interrupt cold openings. Personalized short videos. Delivering coffee when you visit.

Example: The 'Too Honest' Email. Subject: "I don't know what to write here." Body: "Hey [Name], I've rewritten this email four times trying to sound clever, and it's exhausting. So here's the truth: I think we can help with [specific problem]. If I'm wrong, tell me I'm wrong and I'll leave you alone. If I'm right, let's talk for 10 minutes. Deal?" Reply rate: 40%.

That's Level 2: a little courage, big results.

Posture for SDRs vs. Closers

Posture looks a little different depending on your role.

For SDRs, posture is loud and fast. It's in the first five seconds of a cold call, the tone of a voicemail, the subject line of a cold email. It's what keeps you from sounding like a robocall with a heartbeat.

For closers, posture is calmer and deeper. It shows up when you lead a second or third meeting with quiet confidence, when you can talk about money without flinching, when you hold your ground when a buyer tries to drag you back into "just send me a quote."

Same spirit. Different temperature.

SDR posture kicks the door open.

Closer posture keeps you in the room.

LEVEL 3 — Boldly Stupid

Moves that make people say: "Ohhh... you're different."

The Legend of Dr. Ben Dover. A rep created an alter-ego proctologist with lab coat, pocket protector, Coke-bottle glasses, and rubber gloves in his pocket. Nurses rolled their eyes, surgeons made jokes—and he became the most loved rep in the region because he brought levity into a high-pressure environment.

The Cake With the Phone Number. "If you slice this cake before calling me, the guilt will be unbearable." Meeting booked.

The Giant Inflatable Flamingo. Prospect calls himself "Chief Flamingo Wrangler" on LinkedIn; a giant flamingo shows up with "Every flamingo wrangler needs backup." Phone rings within an hour.

That's courage + personality + creativity. You're not trying to impress. You're trying to connect. And connection closes.

LEVEL 4 — Beautifully Stupid

This isn't for everyone. This is folklore level: fully committed, unforgettable, still talked about years later—and always with purpose.

Reverse practical joke. A rep joins a hospital's prank culture with chocolate staplers and bread mousepads, becoming "one of them" instead of "another vendor."

Personalized comic strip. Buyer as superhero saving their org; final panel says "Book a meeting or this superhero gets it." Meeting booked, deal closed, comic still on display.

Full character personas. "Chief Encouragement Officer" with a sign that says "Official Encouragement Provider—Free Refills." "Sales Therapist" opening with "Before we talk business, I need to hear about your emotional wounds from past vendors." Within minutes they're into real pain points.

This is posture at mastery: strategy disguised as fun. The reps who play at this level aren't chasing approval. They're building memories. They're willing to risk an eye-roll to earn a relationship.

The Posture Test

If your prospect met five reps this week, would you be the one they remember?

If yes, posture is doing its job.

If not, you need more stupidity—not louder, not dumber, not desperate. Just more human. More courageous. More unexpected. More you.

Posture isn't trying to be different.

Posture is having the guts to be different.

There's a huge difference.

Your New Job: Make Their Day Less Boring

Here's something most reps never think about: Your buyers are having a terrible day. Not because of you (yet). Because of everything else: inbox full of urgent nonsense, calendar packed with meetings that could've been emails, boss asking for updates on things that don't matter, vendors sending "just circling back" messages.

Your job isn't just to sell. Your job is to be the highlight of their day. The email that makes them laugh. The call that doesn't feel like work. The follow-up that shows you actually listened. The moment they think: "Finally, someone who gets it."

When you bring stupid energy—creative, bold, human energy—you're not just opening doors. You're giving people a reason to look forward to your outreach.

And when people look forward to hearing from you? Everything gets easier.

AI Assist: Stupid at Scale

AI is the posture multiplier. It takes the creative ideas you'd never have time to execute and makes them possible in minutes. Here are four ways to use it—and one rule that governs all of them.

The personalized image. You just had a great call with a VP who's a huge Notre Dame fan. You hang up and open an AI image tool: "Create a Notre Dame offensive coordinator who looks like Lou Holtz coaching his team on a play called 'Cover 2 Pipeline Defense.' Put the prospect's company name on the jerseys." Five minutes later you drop that image into a follow-up email that says only: "Saw this and thought of our conversation. No rush—just made me smile." No CTA. No ask. He's smiling before he reads a word—and he forwards it to his entire team.

The impossible-to-ignore door opener. You've called a prospect eight times and can't get through. Pull their LinkedIn and their company's latest press release, then ask AI to generate a custom image, a fake "wanted poster" with their company logo, or a one-panel cartoon about their industry. Attach it to a three-line email: "I made this for you. Took me longer than I'd like to admit. Worth a five-minute call?" People respond to effort, and AI lets you create it without losing your afternoon.

The posture correction tool. After a tough call, tell AI what happened and ask it to rewrite your follow-up so it sounds "grounded, unhurried, and indifferent to outcome." If the result still reads like "just circling back," delete it and start over. What survives is usually short, human, and confident. This isn't AI writing your emails—it's AI catching your posture drift before the prospect does.

The Stupidity Filter. Before you send anything—email, voicemail script, LinkedIn message—paste it into AI and ask one question: "Does this sound needy, defensive, or like I want something?" If yes, rewrite. If still yes, don't send it. Three seconds, and it will save you from yourself on your worst days.

The rule: AI doesn't make you more interesting. It reveals whether you were paying attention in the first place.

Where Posture Fits in the Journey

You now understand posture—the spirit, energy, creativity, and humanity that separate memorable reps from forgettable ones.

But posture isn't the system. It's the fuel.

You can have all the humility, silence, questions, listening, and posture in the world... but if you don't know your stuff? You lose credibility instantly.

That's why the next chapter covers PIC Knowledge: Product, Industry, Competitive. The three categories of knowledge that make you the smartest, most valuable voice in any room.

Posture is the heart.

PIC Knowledge is the brain.

And together, they prepare you for what comes next.

Your Assignment: Day 5 — Bring Stupid Energy

Pick one Level of Stupidity and execute it this week:

Level 1: Send a handwritten note or fun image to a prospect.

Level 2: Record a 15-second personalized video instead of "just checking in."

Level 3: Do something bold—AI-generated image, creative voicemail, unexpected gesture.

Level 4: Join their world in a way that makes you unforgettable.

Track what happens. Watch how people respond when you bring humanity, creativity, and courage to your conversations.

This is where selling stops feeling like work and starts feeling like connection.

You can learn every framework in this book, but if you don't fix your posture, you'll keep losing to competitors who did.

The data is clear: teams that train on posture and hold themselves to it see 30–50% improvement in show rates and significantly fewer stalled deals. Not because they're more aggressive—because they're more respected.

There is no version of sales success that includes weak posture. None.

If you need the deal, the prospect can feel it. If you're afraid to ask a hard question because you don't want to lose the meeting, you've already lost. If you chase, beg, discount, or "just check in" because you're anxious—you are advertising that your pipeline is empty and your solution isn't worth what you're asking.

Not sometimes. Always.

Let me remove any ambiguity: desperation kills deals.

Day 5 begins now.

CHAPTER 6

PIC Knowledge

Your Brain Is a Stock Price

Let's start with a sentence that will either inspire you... or irritate you:

Your brain is a stock price.

Right now, it is either going up or it is going down. There is no flat line.

If your brain were a stock ticker, would the scroll under your name read: "SULLIVAN INC—UP +3.7% TODAY ON STRONG LEARNING MOMENTUM"?

Or would it look more like: "SULLIVAN INC—DOWN -4.3% AFTER ANOTHER WEEK OF COASTING AND WATCHING REELS ABOUT CAPYBARAS"?

Here's the truth almost nobody tells salespeople: your value in the marketplace is directly tied to your willingness to keep learning. Not your charm. Not your personality. Not your "gift of gab" (which, by the way, is usually a curse). Your value rises when your knowledge rises and drops the moment your learning stops.

Most reps hit that point the second onboarding ends and the badge hits their lanyard. They sit through product training, memorize the pitch, get their laptop and territory, shake hands, grab a company pen, and congratulate themselves like they just graduated Navy SEAL training. Then they coast. And they coast hard.

The Myth of Experience

One of my favorite moments is when a rep proudly announces, "I've been doing this for 20 years."

You know what that means eighty percent of the time?

They've been doing Year 1... twenty times.

They learned just enough to survive. Then they stopped. Then they built a story to defend the stopping. The longer someone has been in the same role, the more likely they've become an expert in their own comfort zone—not in their craft.

Experience is good. Curiosity is better.

The marketplace will beat experience with innovation every single time.

The World Is Moving Faster Than Your Comfort Zone

Think back five years. Would you honestly have predicted: AI writing better prospecting emails than humans, buyers researching you before you've ever heard of them, product cycles updating every quarter, competitors popping up like Starbucks locations?

No chance.

Everything is speeding up: your industry, your customers, your competitors, your tools, your product, your prospects—your entire environment. But most reps are still selling like it's 1999. They learned a pitch, fell in love with it, and now cling to it like a life raft even though the ocean has completely changed.

If you haven't learned anything new this month, your customers have already started to outgrow you.

Why Salespeople Really Stop Learning

The problem isn't time or resources or even knowing where to start. Reps stop learning because they believe two dangerous lies.

Lie #1: "I know enough." No, you don't. Neither do the best reps in your company. The second you believe you know enough, your growth curve flatlines and your stock price quietly slips.

Lie #2: "Learning takes too long." That might have been true when you needed conferences, thick manuals, or full-day trainings. Now you have podcasts, summaries, AI explainers, customer call transcripts, LinkedIn, and competitive breakdowns delivered to your phone like DoorDash for your brain. We live in the easiest era in human history to get smarter quickly.

The Coaster vs. The Climber

You already know both types.

The Coaster is nice, friendly, predictable, reliable. They hit quota when the wind blows the right direction. They know their product "well enough," attend the meetings, nod at the right times, and fly under the radar. Their brain stock ticker drifts downward like a melting ice cube.

The Climber is different. They ask "dumb" questions other reps laugh at. They linger around top performers, take notes in meetings, and ask their manager for feedback. They read. They listen. They experiment. They learn something new every single week. Their ticker moves one way: up, up, up.

Climbers rarely start as the most naturally gifted people on the team. They just invest in their intelligence.

Coasters treat learning as optional.

Climbers treat learning like oxygen.

The Knowledge Gap Your Buyer Can Feel

Your buyer will never say this out loud, but they think it: "I can tell when a rep hasn't learned anything new in years."

They feel it in your answers and in your questions. They hear it in your outdated examples. They sense it when you clearly don't understand their world, when you dance around competitive comparisons, when your value feels stale. Buyers today aren't patient. If you don't bring new insight, they quietly label you as replaceable.

The opposite is also true. A rep who brings thoughtful questions, current context, industry awareness, and competitive intelligence stops being seen as "a salesperson" and starts being treated like a partner.

Your brain is your real territory.

Not your region, ZIP code list, vertical, or account roster. Your brain, your curiosity, your discipline, your learning habit, and your willingness to stay sharp—that's the one territory nobody can steal.

PIC Knowledge: The Three Pillars

Think of this chapter as a performance-enhancing knowledge plan—no needles, no creams, just legal, compounding intelligence. PIC stands for:

Product knowledge

Industry knowledge

Competitive knowledge

Those three pillars have been around since selling began. What changed is the environment. You're dealing with more tools, more information, and far more noise than reps did twenty years ago. If you try to learn the old way—sporadic trainings, dusty manuals, random blog posts—you will get out-learned by anyone with a browser and an AI window.

Product Knowledge

In the 90s, product knowledge was simple: learn the product, memorize the features, recite the benefits, and try not to embarrass yourself. Today your product evolves faster than your company's Christmas-party budget.

You've probably had that moment where you stride into a meeting confident, only to hear, "With the update last Thursday, does this integrate with our workflow now?"—and you feel your soul leave your body.

Product knowledge now means adaptability. You have to keep pace with new releases, micro-features, UI changes, integrations, roadmap shifts, and support tickets that expose real-world problems.

The good news: with modern tools, staying sharp no longer requires hours a day. Use AI to summarize product sheets for different audiences. Mine your support logs to see where the product surprises or disappoints customers. Schedule a monthly 15-minute "What's new?" chat with your product team. Record your demos and study what buyers ask—when the same question shows up five times, that's a learning assignment.

Industry Knowledge

Product knowledge answers "What does this do?" Industry knowledge answers "What kind of world is my buyer trying to survive in?"

Buyers don't just want a feature expert or a polished demo; they want someone who understands their pressures better than the last ten reps who hit their inbox. Industry knowledge gives you the right to ask deeper questions—the kind that make prospects pause and say, "No one's asked me that before."

Every Monday, have AI generate a one-page brief on your main industry: trends, risks, regulatory changes, buying patterns. Curate your LinkedIn feed by following analysts, thought leaders, competitors, and key executives in your vertical. If your team records calls, search transcripts for words like "workflow," "staffing," "budget freeze," "burnout." When certain themes keep appearing, you're staring at the real problems your buyers wake up thinking about.

Competitive Knowledge

Most reps treat competitors like Voldemort—names they'd rather not speak. Top reps do the opposite. They understand competitors so well that objections feel familiar, not threatening.

The goal isn't to insult rivals; it's to understand what your buyer is comparing you to so you can position yourself clearly and confidently.

Ask AI to outline your top competitors, how they position themselves, who they serve best, and where they're likely strong or weak. After deals close, ask customers who else they evaluated, what they liked about those options, and what almost pulled them away from you. Watch what rivals brag about on LinkedIn—product launches, partnerships, big wins, hiring waves.

When you finally talk competitors with a buyer, you don't need to say "They suck." Professional posture sounds like: "They do a solid job for companies who care most about A and B. Where we consistently see customers choose us is C, D, and E." You acknowledge their strengths, highlight your edge, and keep the conversation focused on fit instead of mud-slinging.

The Weekly PIC Sprint

Understanding PIC is one thing; staying sharp week after week is another. PIC isn't onboarding. It's not something you cram the night before a ride-along. It's a small, repeatable weekly discipline.

Pick Friday morning or Monday morning and block off 30–60 minutes. Label it "PIC Sprint" and treat it like a meeting with your future income. Use that time to: watch or re-watch a key customer call, study a competitor's site or pitch, learn a new feature or update, review industry news, run a focused set of AI questions, or shadow another rep's call.

Your skill improves by inches each week, but inches turn into miles. Over time, buyers can feel the difference.

AI Assist: Turn Your Brain Stock Price Up Fast

AI can make staying sharp brutally easy—if you use it as a tutor, not a shortcut. Ask it for a one-page brief on your prospect's industry each Monday ("Summarize the 3 biggest trends affecting mid-market distributors this quarter and how they show up in a VP of Ops' world"), then skim it before calls. Paste a new product sheet or release note in and have it explain the key changes "like I'm a busy rep who has 3 minutes before a meeting," then ask for three questions you could use with a CFO, an operator, and IT.

After a recorded call, feed in the transcript and say, "Show me where the buyer mentioned metrics, risk, or politics that I didn't follow up on—and suggest better follow-up questions." Or try this: tell AI to play a buyer who just heard your competitor's pitch and push back on yours. Every weak answer is next week's PIC Sprint assignment.

AI isn't there to think for you; it's there to remove excuses for not learning.

Build Your Sales Intelligence Vault

You need a place where your intelligence lives. It can be a Google Doc, Notion page, OneNote, notes app folder, or physical binder.

Use it to store: great questions, industry and customer insights, common objections and strong responses, useful analogies and stories, customer quotes and motivations.

Each week, drop in a few things you learned: a new pattern you noticed, a friction point, a competitor angle, a line that landed well.

If you don't capture it, you'll lose it.

If you do, your value compounds.

The Day I Got Out-Learned (And It Still Stings)

I learned all of this the hard way.

Three years into medical sales, I was crushing quota and maybe believing my own press a little too much. I walked into a meeting with a hospital administrator who liked me and had bought from me before. I delivered my usual smooth, practiced pitch.

She listened, then leaned forward and said:

"Brian, that was a great pitch. But I talked to your competitor last week. They knew about the new CMS reimbursement changes hitting us in Q4. They understood how it would squeeze our staffing budget. They had examples from other hospitals in our system. You didn't mention any of that. Are you still paying attention to what's happening in my world, or are you just repeating the pitch you gave me six months ago?"

Silence.

I had nothing, because she was right. I'd stopped learning. I'd stopped reading the industry updates, stopped asking what was changing in her world, stopped being curious. I was coasting on a pitch that worked last year while my competitor was learning what mattered this year.

I lost that deal. But I gained something more important: the realization that my brain stock was tanking, and if I didn't fix it, my career would follow.

That week I made a decision: every week, no excuses, 30–60 minutes of focused learning about my product, my industry, or my competitors.

Thirty minutes a week is 26 hours a year. Twenty-six hours of learning compounds into expertise. Expertise compounds into income.

That administrator didn't just teach me about CMS changes; she taught me that buyers aren't only evaluating your product. They're evaluating whether you are worth their time.

I never walked into a meeting that unprepared again—not because I was scared, but because I chose to be smarter.

Your Assignment: Day 6 — Start Your PIC Sprint

Block 30–60 minutes this week on your calendar and label it "PIC Sprint." Treat it like a customer meeting. During that block:

Run one AI industry brief for your main vertical. Watch or read one recent customer conversation. Create or open your Sales Intelligence Vault and set up a few sections (questions, industry insights, objections, competitors, stories).

Add at least five items to that Vault: one great question you heard or asked, one competitor angle or weakness you discovered, one industry trend affecting your buyers, one product feature buyers often misunderstand, one objection response that worked this week.

Then ask yourself: "What did I learn this week that made me more valuable?"

If you can answer that question every week, your stock price is rising—and your buyers can feel it. They feel it in your questions, in your answers, and in your confidence.

One day, someone younger than you will join your company and outwork you, outlearn you, and pass you—unless you decide to stay sharp. You can't control your talent, your product, the economy, or your territory. But you can absolutely control whether your brain stock is going up or down.

What you know determines what you earn.

Invest in it.

Day 6 begins now.

PART III
PRECISE ACTIONS: THE 20-DAY SPRINT

CHAPTER 7

Plan Like a Pro

The Day You Take Control of Your Calendar Is the Day You Take Control of Your Income

If there's one universal truth in sales—across industries, across decades, across personality types—it's this:

Salespeople are shockingly bad at controlling their own calendars.

Please don't take that personally. If you're reading this book, you're probably one of the smart ones, the ambitious ones, the "I want to get to the top" ones.

But even YOU... even my elite performers... even the folks who pay me real money for coaching...

Most still wake up every Monday with a blank calendar, a vague idea of what they "should" do, and a deep hope that the universe magically drops opportunities in their lap.

Spoiler: the universe is busy. It's not dropping anything.

The Harsh Truth

Top performers don't make more money because they're better at sales.

Top performers make more money because they're better at choosing what to do every day.

Average reps get 8 hours a day. Top reps get 8 hours a day. Low performers get 8 hours a day.

The difference is this:

Average reps fill the day. Top reps design the day.

One group reacts. One group owns. One group "tries to find time." One group makes time. One group lets the day happen. One group attacks the day like it owes them money.

Why Planning Matters More Than Talent

When I coach sales leaders on what separates their top performer from the rest of the team, they almost always talk about personality:

"She's got this charisma..."

"He's great with people..."

"They just have that IT factor..."

No. Wrong.

The real difference is this:

Top performers plan their days. Everyone else just survives them.

Top performers don't wake up and wonder who they'll call today. They've already decided. Top performers don't guess who they'll visit this week. It's already on the calendar. Top performers don't rely on "I'll get to it later."

Because they know:

"Later" is where sales careers go to die.

The Rocks, the Pebbles, and the Sand

You've probably heard the old time-management analogy: Rocks = big, important tasks. Pebbles = medium tasks. Sand = all the tiny, low-value distractions.

If you fill your day with sand first, you'll never have room for rocks.

Today, here's what "sand" really looks like: inbox grazing, CRM fiddling, driving an hour to see a "warm maybe" because you don't want to make cold calls, spending 20 minutes rewriting a Slack message so it sounds professional, research disguised as procrastination, organizing your desk because "a clean desk helps me focus," waiting in your car because "it's too early to call people," checking LinkedIn to see who liked yesterday's post, turning a 12-minute lunch into a 52-minute lunch because "mental health."

Sand feels productive. It looks like work. It tastes like work. It is NOT work.

And the rocks? Prospecting. Booking meetings. Running discovery. Delivering demos. Asking great questions. Closing deals. Following up like a machine.

That's it. Sales is simple. Not easy—but simple.

Most Reps Don't Know Their Rocks

Ask a rep what their "high-value activity" is, and they'll give you an entire TED Talk.

Ask the same rep how many prospecting blocks they scheduled this week, and you'll usually hear: "Uhhhhh…"

Or better yet: "I prospect when I can."

No, you don't.

There are unicorns. There are Bigfoot sightings. There are people who claim to enjoy kale. But there has NEVER been a salesperson in the history of the world who "just finds time" to prospect.

Time is not found. Time is MADE.

And the reps who make time, make money.

The Monday My Calendar Exposed Me

Early in my career, I had a Monday that should've been a warning sign.

I showed up at 8 a.m. with zero plan. Just a vague idea that I "should probably prospect."

By 10 a.m., I'd: checked email 12 times, reorganized my Franklin Planner for 30 minutes, updated my contact notes for another 20 minutes, sharpened pencils (yes, really).

By noon, I'd made zero prospecting calls.

By 3 p.m., I was in panic mode, frantically calling anyone I could think of.

By 5 p.m., I felt exhausted—but I'd accomplished nothing.

That night, my manager asked: "How many meetings did you book today?"

"Uh... none."

"How many prospecting calls did you make?"

Silence.

She said something I'll never forget:

"Your calendar is a mirror, Brian. And right now, it's showing me a rep who's hoping for success instead of engineering it."

That stung. But she was right.

The next Monday, I did something different: I blocked 90 minutes at 9 a.m. for prospecting. Labeled it "DO NOT MOVE" in my calendar. Treated it like a doctor's appointment.

Those 90 minutes changed everything.

Twenty-three dials. Four conversations. Two meetings booked.

By 10:30 a.m., I'd already won the day.

By Friday, I had eight meetings booked for the following week. My pipeline went from anemic to alive.

Not because I got smarter. Because I stopped letting my calendar happen to me.

Pipeline Math

Here's an exercise I run in every bootcamp. I point to someone and ask: "How many new deals do you want to close this quarter?"

If they're in a complex sale, they might say 4. If they're in a transactional environment, they might say 12.

"So how many meetings do you need to get those numbers?"

They usually guess: "Uh... maybe 15?"

"Great. So how many prospecting attempts do you need to BOOK 15 meetings?"

And suddenly they look like someone asked them to explain Bitcoin to their grandmother. They have NO CLUE. Which is insane—because this is your entire job.

Here's the simple funnel every rep should tattoo on their brain:

Prospecting → Meetings → Proposals → Closed deals

If you don't prospect, nothing else happens.

Here's the math: Most reps convert warm meetings to real opportunities at 20–40%. If you need 15 meetings, and 100 outbound calls = 10 conversations = 2–3 meetings booked, you likely need 600–800 outbound attempts per quarter. Break that down: 70–90 attempts a week. 15–20 attempts a day.

Suddenly the world makes sense. Your income stops being mysterious. You know exactly what must happen this week to hit target.

Prospecting is no longer emotional. It's mathematical.

The Prospecting Power Block

If you want the secret sauce of high performers, it's this:

They lie to their calendar—and then obey the lie.

They put prospecting time on the calendar before the week starts. They put customer meetings on the calendar before customers ask. They put preparation time on the calendar before they have something specific to prepare for.

They don't wait for time. They make it.

Here's the formula: 90 minutes, three times a week. Non-negotiable. Phone only. Zero distractions.

The goal isn't perfection. The goal is volume + courage.

You don't rise to the level of your goals. You fall to the level of your calendar.

Block it. Protect it. Obey it.

AI Assist: Plan Your Week in Ten Minutes

Use AI to turn a messy territory and account list into a simple weekly plan. Paste a CSV export or a bullet list of accounts into an AI tool and ask it to group them by segment, size, and potential, then suggest A/B/C priority tiers and a four-day call pattern. A prompt as simple as "Cluster these 60 accounts by geography and potential and propose a four-day weekly route with two prospecting blocks per day" will give you a draft plan you can tweak in minutes.

If you're a field rep, combine that output with a routing tool like Badger Maps or RoadWarrior so AI decides who and when while routing decides where. A tight route means two to three extra meetings a day.

The point is not to outsource your thinking. The point is to stop staring at a blank Monday calendar hoping time will magically appear. Let the machine do the sorting. You do the selling.

Your Calendar Should Be a Fence—Not a Suggestion Box

The second habit of top performers: They protect their time like it's money.

They're friendly—but ruthless. Helpful—but firm. Flexible—but not flammable.

They don't let random internal meetings bulldoze their prospecting blocks. They don't let unqualified "can you drop by?" requests hijack their day. They don't let low-value noise interfere with high-value priorities.

Top performers follow four ironclad rules:

First: Treat prospecting like a doctor's appointment—if you wouldn't cancel a physical, don't cancel your call block.

Second: Turn off all notifications. You're not a lab rat in a dopamine study.

Third: Tell your coworkers clearly: "Yes, I'm available at 11. No, I'm not available at 9:30." Say it with confidence and they'll respect it.

Fourth: Your calendar is a yes/no machine—if it's not on there, it doesn't exist; if it is on there, you do it.

Weak reps use the calendar for decoration. Strong reps use it for domination.

The "Move the Needle" Rule

Here's a rule that changed everything for the reps and SDRs at PRECISE:

Every day, before noon, move at least ONE deal forward.

That can mean: booking a meeting, advancing a deal, sending a killer follow-up, asking a key stakeholder a question, dropping a proposal, closing something small, re-opening something old.

This guarantees momentum. It prevents stagnation. It gives you daily dopamine from winning.

When you win before lunch, you stop being a victim of the afternoon.

The Rhythm of Champions

Your calendar is a mirror. It doesn't lie. It doesn't flatter you. It exposes you.

The reps who win—the ones who consistently crush quota, stay calm, never sound desperate, have margin in their day, and walk into meetings like they belong there—are not "naturally gifted." They're not smarter. They're not luckier. They simply design their life better.

Most reps live in chaos. Their week "happens" to them. Top performers live on rhythm. Their work has cadence. Their calendar has structure. Their days have flow.

Here's what a rhythmic week looks like:

Monday: Momentum Day. Review your weekly plan. Review your pipeline. Schedule outreach blocks. Confirm meetings. Hit 15–20 prospecting attempts before 10 a.m. You don't "ease into" a week. You punch the week in the face.

Tuesday–Thursday: Execution Days. These are the engine of your business: prospect, book meetings, run meetings, advance deals, send proposals, follow up, deliver value, make noise. These are your volume days—your win days.

Friday: Reset + Rebuild Day. Fridays aren't "take it easy" days. They're refueling days. Clean your CRM. Update your pipeline. Review your week. Prepare next week's list. A great Friday creates a great Monday. Slack off Friday, you show up Monday lost. Win Friday, you show up Monday dangerous.

The Discipline Muscle

Here's the revelation:

Success is not built on adrenaline. Success is built on repetition.

You plan the same way. You prospect the same way. You follow up the same way. You run meetings the same way. You prepare the same way. You close the same way.

Your buyers may think you're being spontaneous. You're not. You're a machine disguised as a human. And machines win.

People love to talk about motivation, grit, mindset, "peak performance." Almost nobody loves discipline. But discipline is the only thing that separates the rep who crushes quota from the rep who has panic attacks three weeks before the quarter ends.

Discipline doesn't mean perfection. It means consistency. It means you do what you said you'd do, even when you don't want to—especially when you don't want to.

Motivation is a gift. Discipline is a decision.

Show me your calendar and I'll predict your income.

The Daily Question That Changes Everything

Here's a simple exercise that rewires your days:

At the end of every day, ask yourself:

"What did I do today to make tomorrow easier?"

It could be: pre-building tomorrow's call list, researching a new account, preparing slides, scheduling a follow-up, sending a killer recap, cleaning your inbox, mapping your route, rehearsing a tough close, practicing an objection.

Tomorrow is easier when today is intentional.

Top performers reduce friction. Everyone else piles it up.

The Real Payoff of Planning: Confidence

Planning doesn't just make you productive. It makes you confident.

When you walk into a meeting knowing you've already prospected, prepped, researched, built momentum, and moved three deals forward... you walk different. You talk different. You ask different. You close different.

Confidence isn't something you wait to "feel."

It's something you earn—through structure.

Your Assignment: Day 7 — Design Your Week

Open your calendar right now and do four things:

1. Block three 90-minute Prospecting Power Blocks for next week. Label them "DO NOT MOVE." Treat them like doctor's appointments.

2. Do the Calendar Autopsy. Look at your last two weeks and label every activity as High-Value, Medium-Value, or Sand. Be brutally honest.

3. Calculate your pipeline math. How many deals do you need? How many meetings? How many prospecting attempts? Write it down.

4. Commit to the "Move the Needle" rule. Every day before noon, move at least one deal forward.

Your calendar is either working for you or against you. After this week, it works for you.

Day 7 begins now.

There's a type of seller who's always busy but never winning.

They have a full calendar. They're sending emails. They're "working deals." They tell their manager they're "in the mix" on a bunch of opportunities.

But when you look at their pipeline, nothing's moving. Deals are aging. Meetings don't convert. The forecast is fiction.

This is what happens when activity replaces intention.

Being busy isn't a strategy. Making calls isn't prospecting if they're the wrong calls. "Following up" isn't selling if there's no clear next step.

The sellers who win don't work more hours. They work fewer hours on higher-value activities—because they planned before they dialed.

If your calendar is full and your pipeline is empty, you don't need more effort. You need more discipline.

Prospect Like a Champion

Why Prospecting Isn't Dead (But Wimpy Prospecting Is)

In Chapter 7, you protected blocks on your calendar for prospecting. This chapter is about turning those blocks into money.

If you want the truth—the truth that every sales rep secretly knows but spends their entire career trying to avoid—it's this:

You cannot outsell an empty calendar.

You cannot relationship-build your way around a dead pipeline. You cannot close deals you never got a chance to open.

Prospecting isn't one part of your job. Prospecting is the job.

Everything else—the demos, the proposals, the pricing calls, the negotiation—those are luxuries you earn after you prospect.

And if you're reading this thinking, "Sully, that sounds harsh..."

Good.

Because this is the chapter that helps you become the salesperson the competition fears. This is where your career stops being accidental. This is where the excuses melt and the math takes over. This is where you start your climb.

The Big Lie: "Cold Calling Is Dead"

People love to repeat this like it's gospel. It's almost always said by someone who hasn't made a call in eight years.

Cold calling isn't dead.

Bad calling is dead. Lazy calling is dead. Fear-based calling is dead. Robot calling is dead. "Hi, my name is..." calling is dead.

But great prospecting—human, confident, well-planned prospecting—is more alive than ever.

How do I know? Because at PRECISE Performers, my team makes 300–500 outbound dials every single day for clients in dozens of industries. Every day we see what buyers respond to, what shuts them down, what gets meetings, what gets deleted, what sparks opportunity.

We're not guessing. We're not theorizing. We're in the fire daily.

Prospecting isn't dead. But the old version of you might be. And that's a great thing, because this chapter is where we rebuild you.

Prospecting Is a Math Problem, Not an Emotional Problem

Most reps make prospecting emotional: "Ugh, I'm not feeling it today..." "I need to get organized first..." "I'll do it after lunch..."

Nope. That's amateur hour.

Professionals don't treat prospecting like a mood. They treat it like math.

You already know the formula from Chapter 7: Prospecting $\rightarrow$ Meetings $\rightarrow$ Proposals $\rightarrow$ Closed Deals. Once you see the math, you stop fearing the work. Prospecting stops being an emotional fog you hope to navigate and becomes a simple multiplication table.

You don't have to feel brave. You don't have to wait for motivation. You don't have to "get in the zone." You just have to hit the numbers.

Outcomes are unpredictable. Inputs are 100% in your hands.

The input is your job.

The Calendar Tells the Truth

If you've been in sales longer than 14 minutes, you already know this: your calendar tells the truth. Your pipeline doesn't.

The pipeline is a wishlist. The calendar exposes you.

Are you a seller or an inbox manager? A hunter or a professional "follow-up" artist? A creator of opportunity or a really nice person with an empty commission check?

If you want to know the truth about your future income, you don't look at closed deals, pipeline stages, or the number of "good conversations." You look at: meetings set, meetings conducted, meetings advanced.

If those numbers aren't growing, neither is your life.

Activity Creates Meetings. Meetings Create Money.

People overcomplicate sales. They tell themselves:

"I need a better CRM." "I need a bigger territory." "I need a better product." "I need more leads." "I need more trade shows." "I need better messaging."

No, you don't. You need more conversations.

Sales is a simple equation:

Prospecting → Meetings → Proposals → Closed Deals → Money → Lifestyle

If the first arrow breaks, the entire machine collapses.

Your income is not a reflection of your talent. It's a reflection of your activity.

Not your potential. Not your intentions. Not your busyness. Your activity.

That's the big secret of elite salespeople: they prospect before they feel ready.

You don't prospect because you're confident. You become confident because you prospect.

The Multi-Product Trap

If you sell only one thing, life is simple. But most reps don't.

You might have Product A, Product B, Product C, Product D. Each one has its own ideal buyer, buying trigger, objection profile, conversion rate, and sales cycle length.

So when reps say, "I'm prospecting," but have no idea which product they're prospecting for, they're not prospecting. They're wandering.

I worked with a rep who sold both SaaS subscriptions and consulting services. She treated them as "one pipeline." Result? Neither got enough attention. Her SaaS deals stalled because she wasn't booking enough demos. Her consulting deals died because she wasn't nurturing relationships.

Once she separated them and assigned weekly targets to each—10 SaaS calls, 5 consulting touchpoints—her pipeline doubled in six weeks. Same talent. Same market. Different math.

Top performers have pipelines inside their pipeline.

They don't prospect "in general." They prospect with intent.

Email Does Not Equal Prospecting

Let me say something that 90% of reps won't like:

Sending 20 cold emails is not 20 prospecting attempts. It's one attempt disguised as productivity.

Think about your own inbox. When you open it in the morning, how many cold emails do you delete without reading? Ten? Fifteen? More?

Do you ever think, "Oh boy, a cold email! I hope it's a vendor trying to sell me something"?

Of course not. And your prospects don't either.

If your "prospecting strategy" is hiding behind your keyboard because it protects your ego, you're not prospecting. You're avoiding. You're not being strategic. You're being scared.

You're not a hunter. You're a keyboard warrior with Wi-Fi.

Keyboard warriors get dominated by reps who aren't afraid to hear "no"—on the phone or face-to-face. Rejection is the price of admission. If you avoid rejection, you avoid success.

Why Prospecting Feels Hard (And Why That's Your Advantage)

Let's be honest: prospecting terrifies people. It triggers every insecurity a human can have.

Prospecting requires: interrupting strangers, risking rejection, processing judgment, sounding confident, asking for time, leading the conversation, staying composed.

That's not easy work. And that's exactly why it's your opportunity.

Most salespeople simply won't do it consistently. They'll plan to do it. They'll schedule it. They'll think about it. They'll prepare for it. They just won't do it.

Which means the market isn't saturated. The market is wide open—for the brave. The fear you feel? Every rep feels it. The difference is whether you act anyway.

Our SDRs at PRECISE Performers aren't fearless. They're consistent. They're trained, practiced, coached, prepared, and resilient. They get punched in the face by rejection every day—and keep dialing. That's why they win.

Posture Before Technique

We're not going into the full PRECISE mechanics yet—that comes later. Right now, what matters is this: everything you've learned so far about posture, curiosity, and listening is amplified during prospecting.

Prospecting demands: confidence, clarity, energy, pace, warmth, brevity, humor, human tone, a tiny bit of swagger.

Technique matters, and we'll get there. But posture is the fuel. Buyers don't respond to robots. They respond to people.

Prospecting is the part of selling where you have five seconds to make someone not hate you. Your energy, voice, and presence are what carry you through those five seconds.

The Morning I Almost Quit Prospecting

Early in my Welch Allyn days, I had a Monday morning prospecting block that nearly broke me.

I sat at my desk with a list of 30 names and stared at the phone like it was a venomous snake.

I spent 45 minutes "organizing my CRM." I rewrote my opener three times. I walked to the break room for coffee I didn't want. I checked my email. I updated a pipeline note that didn't need updating.

By 10:30 a.m., I'd made zero calls.

Then my manager walked by and said, "How many you at?"

"Uh... I'm still warming up."

He didn't yell. He didn't lecture. He just said:

"Sully, the worst call you make today is still better than the best call you never made."

That hit me.

I stared at the phone for another ten seconds. Then I dialed the first name.

Voicemail.

I dialed the second. Hung up on.

Third call? Conversation. Not a great one, but a real one.

By call seven, I had a meeting booked for Thursday. By the end of the hour, I had three meetings and a momentum I couldn't explain.

I realized something that day: the fear doesn't disappear after the first call. But the paralysis does.

You don't wait to feel brave. You dial until bravery shows up.

Action kills fear faster than thinking ever will.

The Three Enemies: Fear, Fiction, and Feelings

Most salespeople know exactly what they should be doing. They're not confused or under-trained. They're stuck because something inside them resists doing the one activity that changes everything.

You will always face three enemies:

Fear: The Invisible Hand That Steers Your Day. The phone feels like it weighs 200 pounds when you haven't been using it. Fear creates busywork. Busywork creates fake productivity. Fake productivity creates empty quotas. Here's what pros internalize: rejection isn't personal—it's math. If you need 200 calls to land 15 meetings, then 185 rejections are simply part of the recipe. Rejection is not the enemy. Rejection is the ingredient. Getting mad at rejection is like getting mad at flour for being in a cake.

Fiction: The Stories You Tell Yourself. "People don't answer the phone anymore." "Decision-makers hate being called." "No one wants a cold call." The inconvenient truth: the only reason you think cold calls don't work is because you don't make enough of them for the math to kick in. Cold calls "don't work" in the same way treadmills "don't work." They don't work if you don't get on them.

Feelings: The Trap That Keeps Reps Stuck. "I don't feel ready." "I don't feel confident." "I don't feel in the right headspace." Feelings are liars. Elite salespeople understand something that changes everything: action creates feelings, not the other way around. Confidence doesn't precede the call. Confidence is produced by the call. Momentum isn't a mood. Momentum is manufactured by motion.

The Cure: Micro-Motions

One simple habit can change everything: when you feel resistance, commit only to the next micro-action, not the whole mountain.

Don't commit to 50 calls. Commit to dialing the first one. Don't commit to an entire hour. Commit to one name on the list. Don't psych yourself out with outcomes. Commit to making contact.

Once you make one call, the second is easier. By the tenth, you're in rhythm.

Every rep knows this feeling: the call you fear most turns out to be nothing. You build it up in your head, imagine the worst, procrastinate... then finally dial and hear, "Sure, we can talk."

Humans make terrible psychics. Stop predicting doom. Start making calls.

The SDR Who Went From 1 Meeting a Week to 12

One of my SDRs—let's call her Maria—joined PRECISE Performers terrified of the phone.

Week 1: she made 80 calls and booked 1 meeting. She was miserable.

Week 2: we didn't change her script. We changed her mindset.

We told her: "Your job isn't to book meetings. Your job is to make 100 calls. Meetings are the side effect."

That subtle shift changed everything. She stopped treating each call like life-or-death and started treating it like repetitions at the gym.

Week 3: 12 meetings booked.

Same script. Same list. Same phone. Different math in her head.

When I asked what changed, she said: "I stopped hoping to avoid rejection and started expecting it. Once I made rejection normal, the yeses became bonuses instead of surprises."

Rejection isn't failure. Rejection is inventory.

That's what happens when you submit to the math instead of your feelings.

The Two Biggest Lies That Sabotage Prospecting

Lie 1: "I need to research before I reach out." No, you don't. You need a list, an opener, a reason, a voice, and courage. Research matters, but research addiction is procrastination wearing glasses.

Lie 2: "I need the perfect script." Scripts are sheet music. They guide you toward the melody. Pros don't cling to the page; they practice until the script becomes the rhythm of their thinking. Bad scripts sound scripted. Good scripts sound conversational. Elite scripts feel like jazz—natural, flowing, adaptive.

You don't prospect because you have the perfect script. You develop your best script because you prospect.

AI Assist: Sixty Seconds Before You Dial

Research addiction is fear wearing a blazer. Kill it with a strict prompt: "Give me only three relevant insights about this company that would matter in a first conversation. Nothing else." If the answer isn't useful in thirty seconds, it doesn't belong in prospecting. You're not writing a thesis. You're earning permission to have a conversation.

After you draft your opener, pressure-test it before you dial. Paste it into AI and ask: "Does this sound confident, neutral, or needy?" If the answer isn't confident, rewrite it. Then ask: "Shorten this so it sounds conversational, not impressive." Do the same with voicemails—most reps leave messages that sound like hostage negotiations. Elite prospecting sounds unimpressed, and AI strips out the ego, fluff, and nervous energy faster than you can hear it yourself.

AI should speed you up, not soften you. If it makes you hedge your words, sound safer, or avoid the phone, you're using it wrong. If it makes you more prepared, more specific, and faster to dial—you're using it like a pro.

The Phone Doesn't Get Lighter

Here's the truth nobody tells you:

The phone doesn't get lighter. You get stronger.

The rejection doesn't hurt less. You just stop flinching.

The fear doesn't disappear. You just stop letting it steer.

One day, someone in your territory is going to outwork you, out-prospect you, and take the deals you were "planning" to go after—unless you decide to move first.

You can't control talent. You can't control territory. You can't control the market. But you can absolutely control whether you pick up the phone.

The reps who prospect consistently become untouchable.

The reps who avoid it become forgettable.

Your Assignment: Day 8 — Make the First Call

Block 30 minutes tomorrow morning. Label it "Prospecting Power Block."

During that block:

Make 10 calls. Not emails. Not LinkedIn messages. Calls.

Track what happens: How many voicemails did you leave? How many conversations did you have? How many meetings did you book?

Then ask yourself: "Was that as scary as I thought it would be?"

The answer is almost always no.

Activity creates meetings. Meetings create money.

Day 8 begins now.

Here's what happens when sellers actually commit:

Teams that adopt disciplined daily prospecting—not occasionally, not when they feel like it, but as a non-negotiable habit— consistently see 40–80% increases in qualified meetings within 60–90 days. Pipeline growth of 50–100% is normal. In organizations where outbound was inconsistent before, pipeline frequently doubles.

This isn't theory. This is data from over 1,200 companies we've trained.

And here's what's uncomfortable about that: the improvement doesn't come from better tools, better leads, or better markets. It comes from behavior finally matching intent.

The teams who don't see results? They're the ones who trained, agreed with everything, and then went back to doing what they were already doing.

You can't read your way to a better pipeline. You have to prospect your way there.

What Happens When Teams Train but Don't Adopt

I need to tell you what I've seen happen—not to the teams that reject this system, but to the teams that agree with it and then don't follow through.

It's a pattern. And it's quieter than you'd expect.

The first two weeks go well. There's energy. Reps use the new language. Managers pay attention. Prospecting picks up. Everyone feels like something has shifted.

Then week three arrives. The calendar fills up. A big deal demands attention. The daily discipline starts to slip—just a little. "I'll get back to it tomorrow."

By week six, the language has softened. The Call Sheets sit in a drawer. The pipeline looks the same as it did before. Managers stop inspecting because there's nothing new to inspect.

By month three, no one talks about the training anymore. If you asked the team what changed, they'd struggle to answer. Not because it didn't work—because it was never given the chance to.

Here's what I've learned: training without reinforcement doesn't fail loudly. It fades quietly. And the teams that let it fade don't get worse—they just stay exactly where they were. Which, over time, is its own kind of failure.

The difference between teams that transform and teams that "attended training" is not intelligence. It's not talent. It's not even effort.

It's simply whether the standards held past the point where holding them became inconvenient.

That's the only difference.

CHAPTER 9

Prepare

Win Before the First Word

There's a moment you can spot—if you've been around this game long enough—where you know exactly who's about to win the call.

It's not when the rep starts talking. It's not when they deliver the hook. It's not even when they ask the first question.

It happens before the call ever begins.

Elite salespeople walk into conversations with a presence average reps can't fake.

Calm. Clear. Dangerous in the best possible way.

And it's not because they're more charismatic, more extroverted, or "naturally gifted."

They win because they do something most reps avoid like cardio: they prepare.

Not the fake kind of preparation—corporate zombies highlighting 42-page PDFs and pretending reading is progress. That's just stress-cleaning with a laptop.

Real preparation is small, simple, quick, sharp, and purposeful. And it changes everything about how the buyer experiences you.

Buyers can feel when you're prepared. They also feel when you're winging it. Most reps are winging it so consistently that "under-researched improvisation" might as well be their job title.

The Two Kinds of Reps

If you've ever hired, coached, or watched reps stumble through meetings they had no business taking, you know there are only two types of sellers:

Those who prepare to win.

Those who prepare to react.

The first walks into calls with intention. The second walks in hoping the buyer will tell them what to do.

One leads the conversation. The other survives it. One walks in calm. The other walks in slightly sweaty. One has a plan. The other has a prayer.

Hope has never once hit quota.

The Amateur's Greatest Hits

Unprepared reps always say some version of:

"I don't want to sound scripted." "I like to keep it loose." "I want it to feel natural." "I'll just see where the conversation goes."

Every one of those sentences translates to the same truth:

"I didn't do the work."

Buyers hear it immediately. They hear the hesitations, the reactivity, the uncertainty. They can tell when you're mentally rummaging through your brain for your next line like it's the junk drawer in your kitchen.

Prepared reps sound like they've done this before—because they have. Not because they memorized a monologue, but because they took a minute to make decisions in advance.

The Real Definition of Preparation

Preparation isn't knowledge. Preparation is clarity.

It's not about knowing everything about the prospect. It's about knowing enough to be intentional.

Here's the entire formula for preparation:

1. Know enough.

2. Decide what you're going to do first.

That's it.

"Knowing enough" doesn't mean you need their favorite team or their dog's name. It means: the name, the role, the company, one likely pain point, one relevant insight, a theory on why today might matter.

Nothing fancy. Just enough to sound like a professional instead of a stranger with a quota.

Then comes the part amateurs skip: deciding what you'll do first. Not everything—just the first thing.

Prepared sellers do not walk in "open to wherever it goes." They already know their first line, their first question, and the first turn in the conversation.

Because they know the beginning, they stay in control of the middle and the end.

A Tale of Two Demos

Let's make this real.

Company A had a rep—call him Jason—who landed a big demo with a regional hospital. It was a chance to displace a competitor they'd been chasing for two years. Jason told his manager, "I've been doing this pitch forever. I know it cold. I'll just feel it out with them."

Translation: "I'm not going to prepare."

He glanced at the slides the night before, skimmed a few CRM notes, and showed up "ready."

Ten minutes into the demo, the CNO asked, "How does this integrate with our existing staffing software? We just rolled out a new system last quarter."

Jason froze. He'd never checked which system they were on. He hadn't talked to product about the latest integration. He hadn't asked himself the simplest prep question: "What are they probably using already?"

He stumbled through a vague answer, promised to "get back" with details, and the energy in the room died.

Three weeks later, they chose the competitor—who had shown up prepared with a one-page diagram showing exactly how their solution plugged into that staffing software.

Same category. Same product quality. Different level of preparation.

Meanwhile, another rep on that team, Erica, treated prep differently. Before her demos, she'd always spend 7–10 minutes: clarifying the objective for the meeting, checking LinkedIn for the key people and their projects, scanning CRM for previous interactions, asking product one question: "Any updates that matter for this type of customer?"

On one call, she opened with:

"Before we jump into the screens, I saw you've been leading that centralization project across your clinics, and you recently moved to X system. I'd love to focus today on how our workflow fits into that reality instead of doing a generic tour. Does that sound right?"

The buyer leaned in. "Yes. That's exactly what we care about."

That deal closed. Less experienced rep. Same product. Better preparation.

Why Preparation Is a Competitive Advantage

Prepared reps project: calm, competence, confidence, professionalism, respect.

Unprepared reps project: chaos, nervous chatter, verbal wandering, over-explaining, under-questioning.

Buyers feel the difference in about six seconds—not thirty.

The first six seconds determine whether the buyer leans in or checks out.

Preparation is what makes those six seconds work in your favor.

Preparation Is Respect

Preparation tells the buyer: "I respect your time." "I'm here for a reason." "I've done the work." "I'm not guessing."

Buyers are allergic to guessing.

Preparation isn't glamorous. It's not a magic trick. It's a quiet discipline that makes every part of PRECISE easier: your opener sounds more confident, your tone carries more authority, your questions come out cleaner, your pacing is smoother, your posture strengthens, your close becomes natural.

Preparation is the multiplier.

Call Objectives: The Part Almost No Rep Gets Right

Most salespeople think they prepare. They glance at LinkedIn, skim an About page, peek at a dusty CRM note from 2021, and tell themselves, "Yep, I'm ready."

But they miss the single most important piece: deciding their objective.

If you stopped a salesperson right before a call and asked: "What exactly do you want this buyer to do as a result of this conversation?"

Most would freeze. One would ramble. One would lie.

They know what they want to do—pitch, explain, present, educate, show slides, talk about themselves.

But that's not an objective. That's activity.

A real call objective is simple:

What do you want the buyer to commit to that moves the sale forward?

Once you know that answer, your preparation sharpens, your questions get cleaner, and your call gets dramatically more effective.

The Cold Call Objective: One Goal Only

On a real cold call, there is only one objective:

Get the meeting.

That's it. Not convince. Not educate. Not pitch. Not build "awareness."

Cold calls that try to do more than one thing do nothing well.

A cold call is a curiosity engine. You're not selling the whole movie—you're selling the trailer.

If the buyer walks away thinking, "Yeah, I'll give this person 30 minutes," you won.

If they walk away thinking, "I fully understand their product now," you lost.

Great cold callers know exactly what success looks like before they dial: "Success = a committed meeting on the calendar."

That clarity changes the tone of your opener, the way you ask questions, how you handle resistance, how you use the hook, how you apply the takeaway. Everything.

When the objective is clear, the call becomes simple.

The Warm Call Objective: Advance the Sale

Now the next stage—the warm call, discovery call, or demo. This is the meeting you earned because your prospecting worked.

Warm calls are not longer cold calls. They are not slide tours. They exist to advance the deal.

What does "advance" mean? It depends on your world: In a two-call close, your objective is a clear yes/no and path to next steps. In a multi-stakeholder sale, your objective is to secure a meeting with additional decision-makers. In a proposal-driven sale, your objective is to get the info to build a proposal and get commitment to review it.

Notice the pattern: warm call objectives are about what the buyer does, not what you do.

Not you presenting. Not you demoing. Not you talking for 30 minutes straight.

The objective is their commitment, their action, their movement.

Good Objective vs. Bad Objective

Bad objective: "I want to show them what we do." It's rep-centered, vague, and passive. It hands control to the buyer.

Good objective: "I want to confirm whether there's a meaningful gap to solve and secure a follow-up with their Director of Operations to advance this." Clear. Specific. Buyer-centered. Forward-moving. Professional.

One creates intention. The other creates rambling.

Once you decide what you want the buyer to do, everything else gets easier: your tone becomes more confident, your pacing slows down, your questions sharpen, your stories become relevant instead of random, your close feels natural instead of awkward.

Objectives kill rambling and wasted time.

Objectives create clarity. Clarity creates confidence. Confidence creates control.

LinkedIn: 45 Seconds of Gold

Most reps "check LinkedIn" the way they check the fridge—open, stare, walk away with nothing. You don't need to stalk people; you need clues.

In under a minute, you can pull: title and seniority (tells you how strategic your questions should be), tenure in role (new = open to change; long = cares about risk and track record), activity and language (the words they use are the words you mirror), background (hints at their perspective), mutual connections or similar customers (instant social proof), projects or featured content ("proud to lead..." are perfect segues for questions).

You are not writing their biography. You're grabbing just enough to sound like you did your homework.

To a VP of Operations with a big rollout: "I saw you've been leading the X rollout across your locations. I'm curious how that's changing what you care about this quarter."

To a Manager newly in role: "Looks like you stepped into this role about four months ago—congrats. What's the one problem you feel the most pressure to solve first?"

Both took less than a minute of prep and immediately separate you from the "Hey, how's your day going?" amateurs.

AI Assist: The 60-Second Call Brief

Before a warm call or demo, paste your CRM notes and the prospect's LinkedIn into AI and ask: "Based on this history and this person's role, what should my one objective be for this meeting, what's the strongest opening question, and what's the one landmine I should watch for?" You'll get a pre-call game plan in thirty seconds that forces you to commit to an objective before you dial—the exact step this chapter says most reps skip.

For warm calls and demos, go one step further. Tools like Crystal Knows analyze a LinkedIn profile and tell you how the person prefers to communicate—direct and fast, or methodical and evidence-driven. That distinction changes your pacing, your tone, and how quickly you push for commitment. A driver wants the short version. An analytical buyer wants the proof. Knowing which one you're walking into is preparation that doesn't show up in your CRM but shows up in your close rate.

Preparation isn't about more research. It's about the right research, done fast enough that it never becomes an excuse not to dial.

Common Prep Traps (And How to Avoid Them)

Trap 1: Over-research. You know their CEO's college, but not what you want from the call. Fix: don't open another tab until you've written your call objective.

Trap 2: Script obsession. You're still editing wording 30 minutes in. Fix: lock version 1 for today; tweaks go into tomorrow's calls, not today's.

Trap 3: "I'll prep later." You start calls cold and promise yourself you'll prep the next block. Fix: schedule a 10–15 minute "prep only" block before your main calling block.

Trap 4: Tool-hopping. LinkedIn → CRM → email → web search → AI → back to LinkedIn, with no calls made. Fix: for each prospect, allow yourself two tools max.

Trap 5: Outcome fantasies. You imagine closing the whole deal today and overload the call with 10 goals. Fix: force yourself to pick one objective that fits this stage of the sale.

The Real Point of Preparation

Preparation is not about being impressive or sounding smart. It's not about knowing everything.

Preparation is about respect.

Respect for your time—you're not winging it.

Respect for their time—you're not wasting it.

Respect for your craft—you're treating sales like a profession, not a hobby.

Your Assignment: Day 9 — Prepare Like a Pro

Before your next prospecting block, spend 10 minutes preparing:

For 3 cold calls, spend 30–45 seconds on each: Check LinkedIn for title, tenure, and one recent clue. Scan CRM for last touch. Write your objective: "Get a meeting."

For 1 warm call or demo, spend 5–10 minutes: Review last meeting's notes. Confirm your objective (what you want the buyer to commit to). Write your first line and first question.

Then make the calls.

Track the difference: Did you feel calmer? Did you sound more confident? Did the buyer engage differently?

The answer is almost always yes.

One day, you'll walk into a call opposite a rep who didn't prepare— and you'll feel the advantage immediately. They'll stumble. You'll lead. They'll guess. You'll know.

Preparation isn't glamorous.

But it's the difference between hoping for respect and commanding it.

Day 9 begins now.

CHAPTER 10
Respect & Trust
The First Six Seconds

If you want to understand why most cold calls die before they ever become conversations, you can measure it with a stopwatch.

Six seconds.

That's all it takes for another human being—gatekeeper, receptionist, operator, assistant, or the decision-maker themselves—to judge whether you are worth listening to, worth redirecting, or worth eliminating from their morning entirely.

Not thirty seconds. Not "once you get into your pitch." Not after your hook. Before your third sentence, the judgment is already made.

That judgment has nothing to do with your product, your company, your title, or how many "years in the industry" you proudly display on your profile. It has everything to do with two things: respect and trust.

Respect = your ability to acknowledge someone's time, workload, pressure, and bandwidth before you ask for anything.

Trust = your ability to sound like a calm, prepared professional—not a needy stranger who wants to steal their morning.

Those two factors decide whether the call goes anywhere at all. And here's what most reps miss: respect and trust begin before the first word you say. They start in how you show up—your tone, pacing, confidence, posture, stillness, and clarity.

Someone can feel within seconds whether you're about to waste their time—or whether you're someone they might actually want to talk to.

Your job in those first moments is to make the other person feel respected, safe, unpressured, a little curious, and still in control. That feeling is what earns you access.

Access is the true currency of sales.

Why Most Reps Lose Before the Conversation Starts

You already know the amateur version of this call:

"Hi! How's your day going. I was hoping you could put me in touch with the person responsible for..."

It's the single most destructive opener in sales. It screams: "I am a cold call. I am unprepared. I'm about to talk at you. You're about to regret answering."

Gatekeepers—we call them innkeepers because their job is to protect the room, not block it—hear that line hundreds of times a month. They're protecting the executive suite, the operations office, the clinical hallway, the plant manager's space, the owner's schedule, the team's focus. They're not being rude. They're doing their job extremely well.

When you sound like the other 99 reps who called that morning, you've lost before you begin. But when you start differently—with calmness, certainty, pace, and professionalism—everything changes. They lean in. They pause. They listen, even if only for a moment.

That moment is the golden window you must own.

What Respect Looks Like in the First Six Seconds

Respect is how you begin. Not with dominance. Not with speed. Not with the frantic tone of a rep who's behind on quota.

Respect sounds like calm pacing, clean wording, no rush, no pressure, clarity, certainty, and professionalism. Respect is when a receptionist hears, "Hi, my name is Brian Sullivan with Company

X—what's your name?" and immediately thinks, "This person isn't treating me like an obstacle."

You wouldn't walk into a restaurant and bark, "Is the chef here?" So why do so many reps treat innkeepers like inanimate objects standing between them and the sale?

Respect changes the energy. It signals maturity, preparedness, and leadership.

People follow leaders far more than they follow product pushers.

The Innkeeper Who Remembered

There was a hospital in the Midwest where one manufacturer's rep had been calling for months. Every time he phoned the front desk, the exchange sounded the same:

"Hi, is Karen there?"

"Who's calling?"

"This is Mike, I just need to speak with her real quick."

You can guess what happened. Because Mike treated these Innkeepers like dogs, he lived in voicemail. His messages never got through. Mike underestimated the power these people have to either help him or deny him.

When our team took over the territory, one of our reps called the same number. She started differently:

"Hi, my name is Lauren with Company X—what's your name?"

"Uh... this is Denise."

"Nice to meet you, Denise. I was hoping you could help me for a moment."

Denise's tone shifted. "Sure, how?"

Lauren continued: "I sent a quick note to Karen last week about an issue a few of your sister facilities are running into with equipment downtime. I don't want to blindside her—what's usually the best way to get 30 seconds in front of her on something like that?"

Denise paused, then lowered her voice a little. "She's slammed in the mornings. If you call after 3 p.m., she usually catches up on calls. And she actually asked about that downtime issue in a meeting last month, so I'll tell her you called."

Two days later, Denise recognized the number, picked up, and said: "Is this Lauren? Hold on, I'll see if I can grab Karen."

Same building. Same role. Same company. Different posture.

Respect turned an obstacle into an ally—and access followed.

What Trust Sounds Like at the Start

Trust is not earned through data. Trust is earned through behavior.

Trust sounds like confidence without ego, directness without force, humility without weakness, and presence without panic. Trust is created by one of the simplest, most powerful lines in the PRECISE playbook:

"I was hoping you could help me..."

That line does three things instantly: (1) It disarms—you're asking, not demanding. (2) It humanizes—you acknowledge their role and authority. (3) It invites participation—they choose to continue: "Sure... how?"

Respect gets their attention. Trust buys you time. Time opens the door.

Everything you want—hook, curiosity, questions, conversation, meeting—depends on passing this six-second audition.

How Professionals Introduce Themselves to Innkeepers

The PRECISE approach starts with calm confidence and genuine respect. It begins like this:

"Hi, my name is Brian Sullivan with Company X—what's your name?"

They answer. You thank them. Then comes the line that changes everything:

"Sue, I was hoping you could help me..."

This phrase works because it acknowledges their authority, invites cooperation, humanizes the interaction, removes confrontation, and builds mutual respect. Most innkeepers respond with, "Sure, how can I help?" Now you've earned the right to move forward.

From there, you link to your purpose: "Sue, I sent a quick note to Joe about a change that might impact your maintenance costs this year. I was hoping you could help me figure out the best way to get 30 seconds in front of him."

You sound like a professional, not a stranger trying to sneak in the back door.

When the Innkeeper Says the Decision-Maker Isn't Available

This is where average reps give up. "He's not in right now." "Okay, I'll try back later." End of call. End of opportunity.

PRECISE professionals don't waste that moment. They gather intel:

"No problem at all, Sue. Just curious—based on what I mentioned, is Joe the right person to start with, or is there someone else you'd recommend?"

That one question turns you from a pusher into a pro. You might learn: Joe isn't the real decision-maker, Joe no longer owns this area, there's a preferred way or time to reach him, someone else must be looped in, or there's an upcoming project or change you should know about.

Even if you don't reach the buyer today, you walk away smarter.

When You Do Get Through — The Transition

When the innkeeper finally says, "Let me put you through," many reps blow it. They celebrate in their head, lose their edge, then answer the phone sounding out of breath or surprised.

You stay in the same calm posture.

When the decision-maker picks up, you don't build fake rapport or talk about the weather. You don't sound rushed or apologetic. You go straight into a confident opener designed to buy you about 20 seconds of oxygen—the oxygen you need to ignite curiosity.

That opener is where the next phase begins.

The Rep Who Stopped Winging It

One of our SDRs, Dan, used to start calls like this: "Hi, this is Dan from Company X. I was just calling to see if you might have a few minutes to talk about..."

By the third word, prospects were already reaching for the eject button. He'd hear "Not a good time" or "Send me an email" before he even got to the point.

We made one change. We gave him a single opener and told him to use it for every call for a week:

"Joe, my name is Dan Carter with Company X—do you have 30 seconds for me to tell you why I'm calling? If it's not relevant, you can tell me so and we'll part ways."

First day: same list, same time of day, same product—but a different opening six seconds. On call three, a CFO said, "Sure, you've got 30 seconds." Dan delivered a tight hook, asked one good question, and booked a 20-minute discovery.

By the end of the week, his "Not interested" reflex responses had dropped, and his "Yeah, go ahead" responses had doubled—without changing anything else in his process.

He didn't become "more charismatic." He just stopped making prospects feel trapped.

The Five Openers That Buy You 20 Seconds of Oxygen

Your opening line decides whether the decision-maker stays or bails. PRECISE sellers choose from a small toolbox of proven openers—each designed to lower resistance, buy time, and create just enough curiosity for the prospect to say, "Okay, go ahead."

All five share the same DNA: respectful, real, disarming, clear, controlled.

1. The Permission-Based Opener (The Workhorse): "Joe, my name is Brian Sullivan with Company X—do you have 30 seconds for me to tell you why I'm calling? If it's not relevant, you can tell me so and we'll part ways." Why it works: polite but not weak, calm but not passive, clear without pressure, gives them control, signals professionalism.

2. The Low-Ego Pattern Interrupt: "Joe, I know this call is out of the blue—do you mind if I take 20 seconds to tell you why I reached out? If not, no hard feelings." Why it works: acknowledges reality, drops the sales "smoke," lowers the emotional temperature. It sounds like something a human says, not a script.

3. The "Good News or Bad News?" Opener (High-Risk, High-Reward): "Joe, you want the good news or the bad news?" Pause. If they say bad news: "The bad news is this is a cold call. The good news is it'll take me 20 seconds to tell you why I reached out, and if it's not helpful, you can hang up." Why it works: disrupts autopilot, creates curiosity, demonstrates confidence and humor. Use with direct personalities—not in ultra-formal environments.

4. The Ultra-Casual Disarm (Field and Trade-Show Friendly): "Joe, quick question—did I catch you between things, or did I just walk straight into something?" Why it works: acknowledges their reality, shows awareness of their time, feels conversational not scripted. Once they answer, you pivot into your hook.

5. The Direct Truth (For Leaders Who Respect Candor): "Joe, I'll be straight with you—this is a cold call. But I think the reason I reached out will make sense in about 20 seconds. Fair?" Why it works: executives appreciate candor, positions you as a peer not a supplicant, signals you won't waste time.

The Takeaway: The Pressure Release Valve

You probably noticed a pattern: every opener contains a takeaway. The takeaway is not optional; it's a core ingredient of PRECISE openers.

A takeaway lowers pressure, increases trust, gives the buyer control, makes you sound more confident, and neutralizes the "I'm trapped" feeling.

Core takeaways PRECISE sellers use: "If it's not relevant, you can tell me so." "If it's not helpful, we can cut it short." "If none of this matters to you, we can leave it there." "If it doesn't make sense, you can hang up."

Without a takeaway, the opener feels like pressure.

With it, the opener feels safe.

The buyer relaxes enough to hear your hook—which is the entire point.

The Six-Second Playback Drill

You don't build a six-second presence by reading about it. You build it by reps.

Pick one opener and one takeaway. Record yourself saying just the opening six seconds on your phone—name, company, and opener up to the first pause. Listen back and ask: do I sound calm, clear, and confident—or rushed and needy?

Tweak your pacing until those six seconds feel like someone you'd actually trust with your time.

AI Assist: Make Your First Six Seconds Sound Like a Pro

AI can turn a weak opener into a confident one before you dial. Paste your standard intro and ask: "Rewrite this so it sounds calm, respectful, and ten seconds long—no apology, no speed, no 'just calling to see if.'" Test five versions, pick the one that feels cleanest, then use it for a week straight.

For innkeeper conversations, script the transition: "I'm about to call a gatekeeper. Give me three ways to say 'I was hoping you could help me' that sound professional and inviting, not sneaky." After calls, feed in recordings or notes and ask: "Where did I sound rushed, apologetic, or like I was asking permission? What should I have said instead?"

AI won't make the call for you, but it will strip out every phrase that kills trust in the first six seconds.

Your Assignment: Day 10 — The Six-Second Sprint

Here's your challenge for Day 10:

1. Choose your default opener. Pick one of the five that fits your market and personality. Pick one takeaway line to pair with it.

2. Script your innkeeper intro. "Hi, my name is ___ with ___ — what's your name? ... [Name], I was hoping you could help me..."

3. Practice out loud. Say your innkeeper intro + opener combo 15 times. Aim for calm, clear, and confident.

4. Run a 30-minute call block. For that block, you are not allowed to improvise your opener. Every call: use your innkeeper intro and your chosen opener word-for-word.

Track three things: Innkeeper success rate (how many times did you get past compared to usual?), decision-maker engagement (how many said "Okay" or "Go ahead"?), and your internal state (did you feel panicked or in control?).

You'll be surprised how quickly your numbers—and your confidence—shift when those first six seconds stop being random.

Because here's the truth most reps never learn:

Prepared sellers don't just know what to say in the middle of a call.

They know exactly how they want the beginning to feel.

They don't hope for respect. They earn it.

They don't demand trust. They project it.

And those first six seconds are where all of that becomes visible.

Day 10 begins now.

CHAPTER 11
Engage with Questions
Use Hooks That Keep Buyers Talking

Your opener landed.

The decision-maker didn't hang up. They didn't shove you into voicemail. Your takeaway lowered their guard.

Now you're standing in the rarest moment in B2B sales:

You have permission to keep going.

It's tiny. It's fragile. It lasts maybe five seconds. But it's enough.

It might sound like: "Alright, sure." "Okay, you've got 20 seconds." "What's this about?" Or, if you're prospecting live: a slight nod, a raised eyebrow, a half-step back that signals, Go ahead.

This micro-permission is the hinge of the entire call. Most reps blow it.

Where 90% of Sales Reps Collapse

If you want to see where cold calls go to die, it's right here—the first breath after the prospect says "Okay."

Because this is the exact moment when the untrained rep thinks: "I have permission! Time to pitch!"

And then out comes the disaster: "Great! So what my company does is—" "We offer a full suite of—" "We have a new product that—" "I'd love to walk you through—"

And the prospect's energy collapses like a bad soufflé.

Nobody wants a pitch right now. Nobody wants features. Nobody wants education. Nobody wants to hear about your company. They barely trust you enough to let you keep talking.

Most reps crash at the exact moment they think they're succeeding.

They confuse permission to speak with permission to sell. Those two things are not the same.

The Problem With Average Reps

If you've ever been on the receiving end of a bad sales call, you already know what average reps do.

They get a sliver of permission and immediately torch the opportunity:

They talk too much.

They talk too fast.

They talk about the wrong thing.

And they talk before the prospect is ready.

This is the moment when defenses go back up, attention drops, politeness expires, and the call ends before it really starts.

Average reps launch into a monologue. Professional reps launch into curiosity creation. That's the difference.

How Pros Think at This Moment

Pros treat the first 30 seconds after the opener like a bank heist.

They are not trying to escape with the money. They're trying to slip quietly past the sensors.

Because once they're "inside" the conversation, they can work.

They know: Power comes later. The pitch comes later. Questions come later. The real selling comes later. Right now they need one thing: a small, clean emotional pull.

That tiny pull buys the next 30 seconds. Which buys the next question. Which buys the next answer. Which buys the discovery. Which buys the meeting. Which buys the deal.

Cold calling is nothing more than a sequence of micro-permissions.

Curiosity is the lubricant that keeps the sequence moving.

The Rep Who Finally Learned to Hook

One of our reps, Alex, used to blow calls right after the opener.

He'd get "Okay, you've got 20 seconds," then immediately launch into:

"Great! So we offer a comprehensive platform that helps organizations streamline their workflow and improve efficiency across multiple departments..."

Eyes glazed. Energy dropped. Call died.

We gave him one Pain Hook and told him to use it for a week:

"Many ops directors we talk to are losing hours every week chasing down approvals that get stuck between departments—which often leads to delayed projects and frustrated teams. If that's not happening on your end, no worries."

First call: "Yeah, that's us. What do you do about it?"

By the end of the week, Alex had booked more meetings than the previous month—using the exact same list, exact same opener, but a completely different hook.

Same rep. Same product. Different 20 seconds after "Okay."

That's the power of a clean hook.

Your Only Job Now: Create One Emotion

When teaching this live, I ask: "What's the one emotion we need to create in the prospect right now?"

People shout: "Interest!" "Confidence!" "Excitement!" "That we can help them!"

All good answers—just not for this moment.

The correct answer is curiosity.

Curiosity is the lowest-friction emotion in human psychology. It doesn't require trust. It doesn't require belief. It doesn't require budget. It doesn't require urgency.

All it requires is a tiny internal reaction: "Okay... keep going."

That's all we're trying to create in the first 20–30 seconds after the opener. If your opener bought you time, your job now is to make the prospect want to give you a little more. Not because you pressured them. Not because you tricked them. Because something you said quietly tugged at their brain.

How Do You Create Curiosity? The Hook.

A hook is not a pitch. It's not an explanation. It's not education. It's not a feature. It's not information.

A hook is a single tight statement designed to make the prospect think: "Wait... what?" "That sounds like us." "We're dealing with that." "Okay, that's interesting—go ahead."

Hooks are the difference between permission to continue and "Hey, I've gotta run..."

When your hook is weak, the call hits a dead end. When your hook is strong, the call flows naturally into conversation.

If you could slap the line on any company's website, it's not a hook—it's wallpaper.

The Three Types of Hooks

You only need three. Three is enough to handle every selling environment:

1. Value Hooks — create optimism.

2. Pain Hooks — create urgency.

3. Name-Drop Hooks — create safety.

Each one earns time in a different way. Each one triggers curiosity differently. Each one matches a different type of buyer psychology.

If the prospect gave you permission, your job is not to talk. Your job is to hook.

The Value Hook — Creating Optimism on Command

Value—when delivered concisely, intelligently, and without hype—creates the cleanest early-stage buying emotion: optimism.

Optimism is the small spark that whispers to the buyer: "If this is true... it could actually help us." It's not excitement. It's not commitment. It's just a small internal lift that says: "This is worth another 20 seconds."

The Template: "The reason I'm calling is that we help [TITLE/INDUSTRY] to [POSITIVE OUTCOME], which often leads to [RESULT OR IMPROVEMENT]."

This template forces clarity, forces brevity, forces you to speak in outcomes—not explanations.

Medical equipment (operations director): "The reason I'm calling is that we help surgical centers reduce procedure bottlenecks and staff burnout—which often leads to faster room turnover and higher case volume without adding labor."

Manufacturing (plant manager): "The reason I'm calling is that we help manufacturing teams eliminate downtime caused by small equipment failures—which often leads to more predictable output and fewer expensive resets."

SaaS for finance teams (controller/CFO): "The reason I'm calling is that we help finance groups automate repetitive month-end tasks—which often leads to closing the books days faster with fewer errors."

What a weak Value Hook looks like: "We have a new product I think you'll like..." "We work with companies like yours to improve workflow..." "We offer a comprehensive solution for your industry..." "We specialize in delivering high-quality service..."

None of these hook anyone. They sound like every other rep. They create zero curiosity. They trigger defensiveness instead of optimism.

The Pain Hook — Creating Urgency in 20 Seconds

If the Value Hook creates optimism—"things could get better"—the Pain Hook creates urgency: "Things might already be breaking... and ignoring it could cost you."

Nothing moves a buyer faster than pain.

When a buyer hears a problem that sounds exactly like their world, two things happen instantly: (1) They feel understood (rare). (2) They feel the cost of not listening (powerful). That's why pain hooks often outperform value hooks—especially with skeptical, overworked, "I've heard it all" prospects.

The Template: "Many [TITLE/TEAMS] we talk to are running into [PAIN]—and it often leads to [NEGATIVE CONSEQUENCE]. If that's not happening on your end, no worries."

Manufacturing / operations: "Many plant managers we talk to are struggling with unplanned downtime because their older equipment is becoming harder to service—which often leads to missed production schedules. If that's not happening on your end, totally fine."

Distribution / dealer sales: "Many distributors we work with say their reps are so overloaded with A-customers that B and C accounts get almost no attention—which often leads to lost share-of-wallet when competitors show up first. If that's not what you're seeing, no worries."

Construction / field services: "Many contractors tell us they're losing hours every week coordinating materials that don't show up on time—which creates expensive idle labor. If that's not something you deal with, no problem at all."

The second someone hears their exact problem described by a stranger, the brain snaps to attention. It's pattern recognition. It's threat detection. It's, "Hold on—how do you know that about us?"

What happens when a Pain Hook lands: "That's exactly what we're dealing with." "Yep. That's happening." "Okay... keep going." "Yeah, we've had some of that."

That's micro-permission again—the buyer signaling you just hit something real. This is where amateurs start explaining and pitching. Not you. You let the hook breathe. You pause. You decide whether to deepen the pain, shift to value, or move toward questions.

Remember: hooks create conversations, not conclusions.

The Name-Drop Hook — Borrowing Credibility in Seconds

If Value Hooks create optimism, and Pain Hooks create urgency, Name-Drop Hooks create safety.

They give the prospect a reason to believe you're not guessing—and that they're not your first rodeo. When you mention a respected peer, competitor, or relevant company you've helped, the buyer's instant reaction is: "If they trusted you, maybe I can trust you too."

The Template: "The reason for my call is that we recently worked with [COMPANY/PEER] who were struggling with [PROBLEM]. We helped them [CHANGE], which ultimately allowed them to [RESULT]. I don't know if any of that applies to your world, but if it does, we might be able to help."

Four moves in twenty seconds: who you helped (credibility), what they were struggling with (relatability), what you helped them achieve (proof), and a takeaway (pressure reduction).

Why Name-Drops work: (1) Collapses skepticism—they stop wondering "Who are you?" and start wondering "How did you help them?" (2) Gives context without rambling—you don't explain your whole offering, just the outcome you created. (3) Shows you know their world—when you cite someone in their industry, another chunk of the wall drops.

Manufacturing / industrial: "The reason for my call is that we recently worked with Titan Fabrication. Their supervisors were losing a ton of time chasing missing work orders. We helped them centralize everything so jobs ran smoother—and it ended up cutting rework in half. I don't know if any of that applies to your setup, but if it does, we might be able to help."

Distribution / dealer sales: "The reason I stopped by is that we work with Allied Supply down the street. They were getting beat to quotes because their counter staff was overloaded. We helped them streamline their process, and it opened up about 20% more selling time. Not sure if your team faces anything similar—but if so, there may be something here."

Construction / field services: "I'm calling because we recently helped IronGate Contractors. Their PMs were drowning in change orders. We helped them tighten up the workflow and it saved them 8–10 hours a week. I don't know if any of that hits home—but if it does, we might be a fit."

The key is not bragging. A great Name-Drop Hook is conversational, humble, and matter-of-fact.

Takeaways in Hooks — Minimal but Essential

By now you've seen takeaways in your opener, your Value Hook, your Pain Hook, and your Name-Drop Hook.

Every hook ends with a pressure release. It keeps you from sounding hungry. It communicates, "I'm here to explore, not force."

And most importantly, it sets up the buyer's natural reaction: "Actually... we might have that problem."

AI Assist: Build Hooks That Don't Sound Like Wallpaper

You don't need 50 hooks. You need one good one, pressure-tested before it hits a real buyer. Take a core pain in your world and tell AI: "Write three 20-second Pain Hooks for a [your buyer's role] who cares about [metric/issue], each ending with 'If that's not happening on your end, no worries.'" Pick the one that feels cleanest. Before you dial, ask AI one more question: "Could any rep in my industry say this, or is it specific enough to make this prospect think I know their world?" If anyone could say it, it's wallpaper—rewrite. Then use it for a week straight.

After that week, paste in your call notes and ask: "On which calls did this hook land, and what exact words did prospects use when they leaned in?" That pattern—the specific language buyers use when a hook hits—is gold. It tells you what to double down on and what to drop.

When you're ready to level up, ask: "Turn this Pain Hook into a Value Hook and a Name-Drop Hook without adding jargon or length," so you always have three angles ready before the prospect ever says "Okay, you've got 20 seconds."

Your Assignment: Day 11 — Build Your Three Hooks

Here's your challenge for Day 11:

1. Write your Value Hook using the template. Add the takeaway: "You may not be dealing with any of that—and if not, no problem." Read it out loud. Does it create optimism? Does it sound like wallpaper, or does it hook?

2. Write your Pain Hook using the template. Read it out loud. Does it name a real pressure your buyers feel?

3. Write your Name-Drop Hook using the template. Pick a real customer. Use their real problem and real outcome.

Then test them: Run a call block using all three hooks across different prospects. Track which one gets the best response—which hook made prospects say "Keep going" or "That sounds like us"?

You don't need to master all three today. You need to find your go-to hook—the one that feels right and works consistently.

Because here's the truth most reps never learn:

Amateurs wing their hooks and wonder why prospects hang up.

Pros script their hooks and wonder why prospects lean in.

The difference between "I've gotta run" and "Tell me more" is 20 seconds of preparation.

Hooks earn conversations. Conversations earn meetings. Meetings earn deals.

Day 11 begins now.

CHAPTER 12

CLEAR Questions

Staying Calm After the Hook

They didn't hang up. They didn't shut the door. They didn't wave you away in the hallway or send you to voicemail.

You used a strong opener. You lowered pressure with a takeaway. You dropped a clean hook.

And the prospect gave you the smallest but most valuable gift in sales: permission.

"Alright, go ahead." "You've got a minute." "Okay... what's this about?"

This is the moment where sales conversations are either elevated— or quietly destroyed.

Why Salespeople Panic Right Here

This is where pressure hits. Now the prospect is listening. Now the rep feels evaluated. Now it "counts."

Most reps react the only way they know how: they start talking. They explain. They describe. They unload features, benefits, history, credentials, and updates no one asked for.

Not because they're bad or lazy. Because their brain has no structure to fall back on.

No structure → panic.

Panic → rambling.

Rambling → product dump.

And once that starts, the buyer's curiosity disappears—even if they stay polite.

The problem isn't confidence. The problem is the absence of a repeatable path.

Why Structure Beats Confidence

Most sales training gets this backwards: confidence does not create control. Structure creates control.

Structure gives your brain somewhere to go when emotions spike. Structure keeps you from filling silence with the wrong words. Structure stops you from defaulting to features just to feel safe.

That's what CLEAR Questions are.

CLEAR is not a script. CLEAR is not a checklist. CLEAR is not an interrogation.

CLEAR is a mental framework—a set of anchors your brain can grab when the conversation starts moving.

Salespeople who use CLEAR don't sound rehearsed. They sound composed. And that difference is everything.

What CLEAR Actually Means

CLEAR is five categories of questions that guide a sales conversation in a natural way:

Currently — what they're doing today

Looked At — what they've explored

Effective — what's working

Alter — what they'd change

Responsible — who's involved or who cares

Five anchors. Five guardrails. Five places your brain can go instead of panicking.

You won't ask all five. You won't use them in order. On a cold call, you rarely use more than one or two. But knowing they exist changes how you behave under pressure.

Why CLEAR Sticks

Leaders who learned PRECISE years ago often say:

"I still use CLEAR." "I taught my whole team CLEAR." "That framework never left me."

They may forget stories and slides. CLEAR stays—because it solves the universal question: "What do I say next?"

When a salesperson has no internal structure, silence feels dangerous. With CLEAR in the background, silence feels manageable.

And when silence feels manageable, curiosity has room to grow.

The Rep Who Finally Stopped Rambling

One inside rep, Jenna, had a pattern.

Her opener and hook were solid. She'd hear "Okay, you've got a minute"... and then panic.

She'd launch into, "So we're a leading provider of..." and talk for ninety seconds straight. Prospects went quiet, then ended with, "Just send something over."

We didn't give her a new script. We gave her CLEAR and only two questions to lean on: one Currently and one Alter.

On her next block, she tried this:

Hook: "Many service directors we talk to are losing hours every week tracking down missing work orders—which often leads to delayed jobs and frustrated techs. If that's not happening on your end, no worries."

Prospect: "Yeah... that's pretty much our life."

Instead of explaining, she asked:

"Got it. How are you handling that today?" (Currently)

Prospect talked for 30 seconds. Jenna listened.

Then she asked:

"If you could change one thing about how that works now, what would it be?" (Alter)

The prospect sighed and said, "Honestly, if we could just see everything in one place so my team isn't chasing paper, that would be huge."

Only then did Jenna give a 25-second convey: who they help, what changes, what happens as a result.

The prospect responded with, "Okay, that's worth a look. Can you talk through this with me and our ops manager next week?"

Same product. Same list. Same rep. The only real change was that she stopped treating silence as an emergency and started using CLEAR as her safety net.

How CLEAR Stops the Feature Dump

When your brain has a question it could ask, it doesn't feel the urge to explain.

Questions slow you down. Questions give the prospect the floor. Questions buy you time without sounding evasive.

Most importantly, questions prevent you from talking about things that don't matter.

You stop guessing what to say. You start responding to what they say.

That's the difference between sounding like a salesperson and sounding like a professional.

CLEAR on a Cold Call — Keep the Objective Small

Right now, you are not in a full discovery meeting. You're not diagnosing the business. You're not solving everything.

You are in a cold conversation with one simple objective: earn the next meeting.

CLEAR questions on a cold call are used lightly and selectively. You may ask one. You may ask two. Some calls, you ask none.

But the moment the prospect says "Yeah, we deal with that" or "That's been an issue" or "That's definitely frustrating"—you've done your job. You've created relevance. You've earned the right to continue.

CLEAR doesn't push the conversation forward. It keeps it from falling apart.

How CLEAR Sounds When It's Done Wrong

Here's what bad CLEAR looks like:

Prospect: "Yeah, we've had some delays."

Rep (panicking with a checklist): "What are you doing currently? Have you looked at other vendors? What's working? What would you change? Who's responsible?"

All in one breath. The prospect feels like they just got pulled into a survey. Their guard goes back up. The call dies.

Now compare that to a disciplined version:

Prospect: "Yeah, we've had some delays."

Rep: "Got it. How are you handling that today?" (Currently)

[Prospect explains.]

Rep: "If you could change one part of that, what would it be?" (Alter)

Two questions. Same framework. Completely different feeling.

Listening for Doors, Not Perfect Answers

Most salespeople ask questions hoping for the "right" answer. PRECISE sellers listen for open doors.

An open door sounds like: "Yeah, that's been an issue." "We've looked at a couple things." "That's not ideal, but it's what we're doing." "I wouldn't say it's perfect." "It depends who you ask."

Those are not objections or stalls. They're invitations.

CLEAR questions are designed to gently surface those invitations—without forcing the prospect to defend what they're doing now.

How CLEAR Actually Sounds in Real Conversations

In real life, CLEAR rarely sounds like you're reading the acronym. It shows up as short, natural prompts.

Currently — Establish the Present State: "How are you handling that today?" "What does that look like on your end right now?" Quick, confident answers usually mean a stable process. Hesitation and "it depends" often mean chaos—good news for you.

Looked At — Are They Passive or Active?: "Have you looked at any alternatives?" "Has anyone else brought this up before?" "No, we haven't" means you're early and may need more education later. "Yeah, we've looked at a few things" means you're relevant and need to differentiate.

Effective — What They Don't Want to Lose: "What's working well with how you're doing it now?" "What would you want to make sure doesn't change?" This is the most underused part of CLEAR—and one of the most powerful. It lowers defenses by showing respect, and tells you what not to threaten later.

Alter — Where Friction Lives: "If you could change one thing about that, what would it be?" "Where does that get frustrating?" "What's harder than it should be?" This framing avoids blame and invites honesty. Even a small answer is enough to justify a next step.

Responsible — Clarifying the Landscape: "Who else is usually involved in decisions like this?" "Who would care most if this improved?" You're not asking who decides. You're asking who cares. That keeps walls down while giving you clarity about the path forward.

The One Mistake CLEAR Protects You From

CLEAR protects you from talking too soon.

The moment a prospect gives a signal—agreement, frustration, curiosity—the average rep jumps to solution mode.

CLEAR-trained reps pause. They ask one more question. They go one level deeper. They let the prospect talk themselves into relevance.

That extra ten seconds often makes the difference between:

"Just send me something..." and "Yeah, let's set up time."

Common CLEAR Mistakes to Avoid

1. Turning CLEAR into a checklist. Asking all five letters back-to-back makes the call feel like an audit. Pick one or two.

2. Skipping Effective and going straight to Alter. If you ask what's wrong before you've respected what's right, people defend their current setup instead of opening up.

3. Using Responsible to chase the "decision-maker" too early. "Who signs the checks?" screams commission breath. "Who would care most if this improved?" keeps the temperature low.

4. Stacking questions without acknowledging answers. When you ask three questions in a row without reflecting anything back, prospects feel interrogated. Slow down. "Got it—that makes sense" buys you permission for the next question.

AI Assist: Practice CLEAR Without Burning Live Calls

Tell AI your industry, your hook, and your buyer's role, then ask it to play a skeptical prospect. Run one CLEAR sequence: deliver your hook, wait for the response, then pick your next question based on what the "prospect" actually said—not a script. The goal isn't a perfect call. The goal is training your brain to reach for a CLEAR question instead of a product dump when pressure hits.

After real calls, paste in your notes and ask: "Which CLEAR letters did I use, which did I skip, and where did I jump to pitching instead of asking one more question?" Over a week of calls, patterns emerge—most reps discover they never ask Effective and overuse Currently. That's the gap that turns "just send me something" into "let's set up time."

CLEAR is muscle memory. AI is the sparring partner that lets you build reps without the cost of learning on live prospects.

When They Ask "So... What Do You Do?"

If you've used hooks and CLEAR well—even lightly—this moment appears almost on its own:

"Okay... so how do you help with that?" "What does that look like?" "So what are you guys doing differently?"

This is where many reps lose the plot. They panic. They over-explain. They rewind their entire website out loud.

This moment is not an invitation to present. It's an invitation to convey—briefly, confidently, and with restraint.

The Rep Who Finally Shut Up

One of our field reps, Marcus, used to walk into facilities and deliver a five-minute monologue about "our comprehensive suite of solutions."

Eyes glazed. Buyers nodded politely. Nothing moved forward.

We gave him one rule: "30 seconds. No more."

His first attempt felt painfully short to him. But when he finished, the buyer said:

"Okay, that actually makes sense. Can you show me what that looks like for our setup?"

Marcus had been trying to earn trust through volume. He learned to earn it through restraint.

Same product. Same buyer type. Different convey.

Two Strong Convey Examples

Finance SaaS: "Based on what you shared, we typically work with controllers who are closing the books later than they want because so much of the process is manual. What we do is help them automate the repetitive parts so they can close a few days faster with fewer errors. If it's useful, we can walk through what that might look like for your team."

Industrial service: "From what you're describing, we usually work with maintenance teams who are constantly reacting to equipment breakdowns. We help them get ahead of those failures so they can plan work instead of living in emergency mode. If it makes sense, we can dig into whether that would actually help here."

Both are under 30 seconds. Both stick to who you help, the problem you solve, and what changes as a result.

If you need to take two breaths and a sip of water to finish your convey, it's too long.

What Success Looks Like in a Cold Conversation

A successful cold conversation is not measured by how impressive you sounded. It's measured by whether the conversation continued.

Did they agree to a clear next step? Is there another conversation? Is it scheduled? Does everyone know why it's happening?

If yes, the call did its job. If no, no amount of clever wording matters.

Most cold calls don't die in dramatic rejection—they die quietly:

"Just send me something." "Follow up in a few months." "We'll take a look." "Reach back out later."

Those are exits, usually created by over-explaining and over-selling too soon.

When you stay disciplined—curious, calm, structured—you're more likely to hear:

"Okay, let's set up time." "I'd want my partner to hear this." "We should dig into this a bit more."

Those are green lights—not because you pushed, but because you didn't.

Your Assignment: Day 12 — Practice CLEAR Under Pressure

Here's your challenge for Day 12:

1. Write one micro-question for each CLEAR letter. Currently: "How are you handling that today?" Looked At: "Have you looked at any alternatives?" Effective: "What's working well with how you're doing it now?" Alter: "If you could change one thing, what would it be?" Responsible: "Who else usually gets involved when this changes?"

2. Build two mini call flows. Flow A: Hook → Currently → Alter → short convey. Flow B: Hook → Effective → Responsible. Say each flow 10 times without a prospect—just to feel the rhythm.

3. Run a 30-minute call block. Commit to using only one CLEAR question per live conversation. After each call, note which letter you used, whether you got an "open door" statement, and whether the conversation continued or stalled.

You don't need to master all of CLEAR today. You just need to prove to your brain that it has a place to go other than "start pitching."

Because here's the truth most reps never learn:

Amateurs talk to feel safe.

Pros ask to stay in control.

The questions you ask—or don't ask—determine whether curiosity grows or dies.

Day 12 begins now.

CHAPTER 13

Convey on a Cold Call

Who the Hell Are You?

By the time you need what's in this chapter, you've already done the heavy lifting.

You opened well. You used a hook that hit a real problem. You took pressure off with a takeaway. You stayed calm and used CLEAR to get the prospect talking about their world.

Now they do what any sane human would do before saying another word about their world:

"Okay... but who the hell are you?"

They might say it directly:

"So what exactly is this?"

"What do you do?"

"Who are you with again?"

Or they might just go quiet until you fill the space.

Either way, they're not going further until two things are clear:

Who are you?

Why should I keep talking to you—even for another minute?

This chapter has one job: show you how to answer that, after CLEAR, in a short, clean way that protects the conversation you've built and earns permission to keep going.

Where This Moment Really Lives

Important: this is not the line you deliver right after your opener, hook, and takeaway.

Early in the cold call, right after the hook, you might give a tiny teaser—one short line like:

"We work with service teams like yours that are dealing with that same kind of chasing."

Then you go straight into questions.

You use CLEAR. You get them talking. They admit where it's not perfect. You earn some trust.

Only after that—once they've opened up a bit—do you get the real "who the hell are you?" moment this chapter is about.

So the sequence for this chapter is:

You've already used CLEAR on a cold conversation.

They've shared some problems in their own words.

Now they want to know who they're dealing with before they keep going.

This is where your post-CLEAR pitch lives.

Step 1: Normalize the Question

First move: let them be right.

When they say, "Who are you exactly?" don't rush, don't get defensive, and don't treat it like an objection. Treat it like the most rational thing they could possibly ask.

"Totally fair question. You shouldn't keep talking to someone if you don't know who they are."

That one line:

Confirms they're being rational, not difficult.

Shows you're not offended.

Buys you a beat to answer on purpose instead of flinching.

You're two professionals deciding if this is worth a few more minutes, not a stranger begging for attention.

Step 2: Use the Simple Formula

Problem → Who → Why It Matters

A good post-CLEAR pitch in this moment is simple. It does three things, in order:

Restate the problem they mentioned.

Tell them who you are.

Tell them why that matters—what pain you remove or value you create.

If you hit those three briefly, you've done your job.

1. Restate the problem (their words)

Start by going right back to what they already told you:

"From what you just shared about..."

"Based on what you said about..."

"It sounds like the big issue is..."

Examples:

"From what you just shared about jobs getting stuck and everyone chasing updates..."

"Based on what you said about closing later than you want because so much is still manual..."

"It sounds like the big issue is cases starting late because equipment isn't ready on time..."

This proves you listened and keeps the focus on their world, not yours.

2. Say who you are in one simple sentence

Then answer "who the hell are you?" in clean, plain language:

"I'm with [Company]. We're a [short category] that works with [companies like yours]."

Examples:

"I'm with Acme. We're a workflow software firm that works with service organizations like yours."

"I'm with Northbridge. We're a training company that works almost exclusively with medical distributors."

"I'm with Apex. We're a maintenance program that works with mid-size manufacturers."

No backstory. No feature list. Just a clear category and clear peer group.

If you have a recognizable reference, you can add one, without flexing:

"We do this with a lot of regional distributors like [X and Y], so we live in that world every day."

One name they recognize is worth ten adjectives they don't.

3. Tell them why it matters (pain solved or value given)

Now finish with the only thing they actually care about: what changes if this works.

Keep it simple:

"We help them [remove the pain] so they can [get the result]."

Examples

"We help them see every job and what's stuck in one place so they spend a lot less time reacting and a lot more time actually running the business."

"We help them automate the repetitive pieces so they can close a few days faster with fewer errors and less month-end chaos."

"We help them tighten turnaround so cases start on time, surgeons are less frustrated, and they can run more volume in the same rooms."

Put it together:

"From what you just shared about jobs getting stuck and everyone chasing updates, that's exactly the world we live in. I'm with Acme—we're a workflow platform that works with service organizations like yours. We help them see every open job in one place so they spend less time reacting and more time running the business."

Problem → Who → Why it matters. One breath. Then back to questions.

Step 3: Stay at the "Keep Talking" Level, Not the "Buy" Level

In this chapter, you're not trying to:

Differentiate from every competitor.

Justify your pricing.

Close for a demo or a meeting.

Right now you're trying to make it feel rational for them to keep answering questions for another minute or two.

So after your Problem → Who → Why pitch, you don't launch into a monologue. You pivot straight back into curiosity:

"That's the world we're in all day. Just so I'm not making assumptions, can I ask you two quick things about how you're set up?"

or:

"That's why I reached out. Would it be okay if I ask you a couple of quick questions to get a clearer picture of how this is hitting your team?"

You're not asking permission for a pitch. You're asking permission for better understanding. That's an easier yes.

The actual meeting ask—the "let's grab 20–30 minutes next week"—lives in the Secure Agreement chapters later. Here, your only job is to keep the conversation alive.

How It Sounds in a Real Call

Here's what this looks like after a CLEAR-style exchange.

You:

"You mentioned your team is constantly reacting—something falls through the cracks, someone screams, and you scramble to fix it. If you could change one thing about how that works, what would it be?"

Prospect:

"I'd just like to see everything in one place so we're not constantly chasing paper."

You:

"Totally get that."

Prospect:

"So who are you exactly?"

You:

"Totally fair question. You shouldn't keep talking to someone if you don't know who they are.

From what you just shared about always reacting and scrambling when things fall through the cracks, that's exactly the world we live in. I'm with Acme—we're a workflow platform that works with service organizations like yours. We help them see every open job in one place so they spend less time chasing and more time running the business.

That's the world we're in all day. Would it be okay if I ask you two quick questions to get a clearer picture of how this is hitting your team?"

Prospect:

"Sure."

Now you're back into questions. No product tour. No slide deck. No "let's put something on the calendar" yet. You've simply answered who you are, proven you were listening, and earned more time.

A Note to Leaders: If You Can't Answer "Who the Hell Are We?", Your Team Has No Chance

One of the most common patterns in companies we train: put twenty reps in a room and ask, "So who are you and what do you do?" and you'll get twenty different answers. Some are two minutes long. Some are full of jargon. Some sound like a Wikipedia page no one would read.

That can't continue.

If your own people can't precisely, consistently answer "Who the hell are we?" in one or two clean sentences, that's not a training problem. That's a leadership problem.

You need to:

Get in a room.

Argue it out.

Decide on the right answer at the level your buyers care about.

Not a paragraph. Not a manifesto. A sentence or two that:

Names who you serve.

Names the main problem space you live in.

Names, at a high level, what changes when things go right.

Once you have it, that answer becomes non-negotiable.

Everyone should be able to say it like a poet—with their own personality, but the same core content. It should come out naturally, not rehearsed.

Build It Yourself—or Let AI Jump-Start It

For years in workshops we built these pitches by hand on flip charts using the same template you saw above. You can still do that—and you should, because the argument is where the clarity comes from.

Template:

"From what you shared about [problem], that's exactly the world we live in. I'm with [Company]—we're a [category] that works with [who you serve]. We help them [remove the pain] so they can [get the result]."

You can also let AI give you a head start:

Grab the best copy from your site—about page, product pages, customer stories.

Paste it into an AI tool and ask for several one- or two-sentence pitches that:

Restate the main problem you solve.

Clearly say who you are (category + who you serve).

End with pain removed or value created.

Most of the suggestions won't be quite right. One or two will make you think, "That's actually better than what we say today."

Pick the best version (or blend a couple), tighten the language with your leadership team so it sounds like you, then:

Practice, drill, and rehearse it with everybody until it's automatic.

Sales, marketing, customer success, leadership—everyone should be able to look a prospect in the eye (or a camera) and answer "Who the hell are you?" in one clean breath.

Make that pitch part of your culture:

Use it to open internal meetings.

Put it on the wall in the sales room.

Bake it into onboarding.

If you, as a leadership team, can't precisely tell a client who you and your company are in a repeatable way, you can't expect your sales team to do it for you.

Give them one great answer. Then hold them accountable for delivering it.

Your Assignment: Day 13 — Build and Practice Your Post-CLEAR Pitch

For this stage of the cold call, keep it short and simple.

Write your base pitch using the formula. "From what you shared about [problem], that's exactly the world we live in. I'm with [Company]—we're a [category] that works with [who you serve]. We help them [pain removed] so they can [result]."

Say it out loud ten times. Aim for under 20–30 seconds. Fix any phrases that feel stiff.

Use it on your next call—only after CLEAR. Don't drop it right after the hook. Wait until they've admitted something isn't perfect and then ask, "So who are you?" or you can feel that question hanging in the air.

Immediately pivot back to questions. "Would it be okay if I ask you two quick questions to get a clearer picture of how this is hitting your team?"

You're not trying to impress them.

You're answering, in one clean breath:

"Here's the problem you told me about."

"Here's the box I live in."

"Here's why that matters to you."

Do that well, and the rest of the call—and the later Secure Agreement and warm-call Convey—gets much easier.

Day 13 begins now.

CHAPTER 14
Indecision
It Isn't Rejection, It's a Moment

Let's clear something up right away.

When a prospect hesitates... pushes back... says "I need to think about it"... or gives you some version of "not now"...

They are not rejecting you. They're doing what normal, intelligent humans do when they feel uncertainty.

Indecision is not the end of the sale.

It's a moment inside the sale.

And how you handle that moment determines whether the conversation moves forward—or quietly dies while you tell yourself, "That was a good call."

Spoiler: it wasn't.

Why Good Salespeople Fall Apart Here

This is one of the strangest things in sales. A rep can prepare well, build respect and trust, create curiosity, ask solid questions, deliver a clean 30-second Convey...

And then the prospect says something like: "We're already working with someone." "Just send me some info." "This isn't a priority right now." "We don't have budget." "Circle back next quarter."

And suddenly... panic.

You'd think this was the first time the rep had ever heard those words. But it's not. They've heard them a thousand times. Yet every time they show up, the response is improvised. Different words. Different tone. Different confidence level. Different outcome.

That inconsistency is what kills deals—not the objection itself.

The Truth Most Reps Don't Want to Admit

Here's the uncomfortable reality. Most salespeople hear the same five objections over and over again:

1. "We're already working with someone."

2. "Just send me some information."

3. "This isn't a priority right now."

4. "We don't have budget."

5. "I need to think about it."

That's it. Not fifty. Not a hundred. Five.

And instead of preparing for those five moments, they wing it every time.

Preparation doesn't make you robotic.

Lack of preparation makes you ramble.

The goal is not to sound scripted. The goal is to sound ready.

What the Best Reps Do Differently

Top performers don't fear objections. They expect them. They know: "If this conversation is going anywhere, some hesitation is going to show up."

So instead of reacting emotionally, they respond deliberately. They've already thought through those five predictable objections, developed clean responses, and practiced them enough that they sound natural.

When the objection shows up, they don't scramble. They slow down.

That's where SHARP comes in.

The SHARP Framework — How to Handle Indecision Without Pressure

When indecision shows up, most salespeople do one of two things: they push harder, or they retreat completely.

Neither works. Pressure creates resistance. Retreat kills momentum.

SHARP lives in the middle. It gives you a calm, controlled way to respond when a prospect hesitates—without sounding defensive, needy, or salesy.

S — Stop

This might be the most important step—and the one most reps skip.

When a prospect says "We're already working with someone" or "Just send me something," the average rep immediately starts talking. Explaining. Justifying. Defending. Selling harder.

That's a mistake. The first thing you need to do is stop.

Not dramatically. Not awkwardly. Just enough to slow the moment down.

Indecision is emotional. Speed amplifies emotion. Pausing reduces it.

A simple pause tells the prospect: "I'm listening—not reacting." That alone lowers tension.

H — Hear Them Out

This is where most objections get mishandled. Salespeople think they're hearing the objection—but they're really just waiting for their turn to respond.

"Send me some information" rarely means "send me information." It usually means: "I'm not convinced yet." "I don't understand this enough." "I don't want to decide right now." "I'm busy and unsure if this matters."

If you respond to the words instead of the meaning, you miss the moment.

So instead of reacting, you acknowledge. Not with fake empathy. Just recognition: "Got it." "That makes sense." "I hear you."

Those three phrases keep more deals alive than any feature ever will.

A — Ask One Smart Question

This is where SHARP separates pros from amateurs.

You don't ask five questions. You don't interrogate. You don't jump back into full discovery mode. You ask one question—designed to clarify, not corner.

The purpose is simple: Find out what's really driving the hesitation.

Good SHARP questions sound like: "When you say it's not a priority, what's taking precedence right now?" "What are you comparing this against?" "What would need to change for this to be worth a closer look?" "Is it more a timing issue—or an uncertainty issue?"

Notice what these questions don't do. They don't argue. They don't defend. They don't push. They invite honesty. And honesty is the only thing that moves the sale forward.

R — Respond (Briefly and Specifically)

Once you understand the hesitation, now—and only now—do you respond.

This is where a lot of reps go off the rails. They respond with too much information, too many examples, too much enthusiasm, a full-blown pitch.

Don't do that.

Your response should do one thing: Address the concern you just uncovered—and nothing else.

If the hesitation was about timing, respond to timing. If it was about relevance, respond to relevance. If it was about risk, respond to risk.

Short. Clean. Human. You're not trying to win an argument. You're reducing uncertainty.

If you feel yourself talking longer than 20–30 seconds, stop. You've already said too much.

P — Pack It With Agreement

This step is misunderstood—and it's critical.

Packing it with agreement does not mean forcing a close. It means confirming alignment. You're simply asking: "Does what I just said make sense to you?"

It might sound like: "Does that line up with how you're thinking about it?" "Is that fair?" "Based on that, does it make sense to keep the conversation going?" "Am I understanding your concern correctly?"

This step does two powerful things: (1) It gives the prospect control. (2) It prevents you from moving forward on false assumptions.

If they say yes, you've earned the right to continue. If they say no, you just saved yourself from chasing a ghost. Either way, you're back in clarity.

The Rep Who Stopped Losing Deals at "Send Me Something"

One of our inside reps, Derek, had a frustrating pattern.

He'd nail the opener, drop a solid hook, ask good CLEAR questions, deliver a clean Convey—then the prospect would say:

"Yeah, this sounds interesting. Just send me some information and I'll take a look."

Derek would say: "Absolutely! What's your email?"

He'd send a perfectly packaged PDF within five minutes. Then... nothing. No response. No follow-up. No meeting.

When we listened to his calls, the pattern was obvious: the second someone said "send me something," Derek treated it like a win and immediately complied.

We gave him one SHARP sequence to use instead:

Stop: Pause, don't rush to agree.

Hear: "Got it, happy to send something over."

Ask: "Just so I don't waste your time, what would you actually want to see in that?"

Respond: Based on their answer, send a targeted overview—not everything.

Pack: "Does it make sense to schedule a quick 15-minute follow-up for next week to see if any of this is worth exploring?"

First call using it: the prospect said, "Yeah, let's do that."

Within a month, Derek's "send something" responses dropped by 60%—and his booked follow-up meetings went up by the same amount.

Derek didn't become more aggressive. He became more deliberate.

SHARP in Real Objection Moments

"We're Already Working With Someone"

This isn't rejection. It's context. The worst move: instantly trying to prove you're better.

Prospect: "We're already working with someone on this."

(S) Pause. **(H)** "Got it—that's what most of the teams we talk with say at first." **(A)** "Out of curiosity, how's that working for you so far?"

[If they say "honestly, pretty well," you know this isn't your fight today.]

(R) "Good to hear. If you're in a good spot, I don't want to disrupt what's working. The only time folks usually talk with us is when something changes—growth, new leadership, or things stop working the way they used to." **(P)** "If any of that ever hits your world, would it be reasonable to reconnect then?"

No pressure. No bashing. Just clarity and a clean exit or future door.

"This Isn't a Priority Right Now" — Full SHARP Transcript

This one feels final, but rarely is.

Prospect: "This isn't really a priority right now."

(S) Stop—brief silence, breathe. **(H)** "That makes sense. Everyone's juggling a lot right now."

(A) "When you say it's not a priority, is that because it's not really a problem—or because other things are just louder at the moment?"

Prospect: "It's more that other things are louder. We do have the problem, but we're dealing with some bigger fires."

(R) "Totally get that. What we usually see is that teams keep this on the back burner until one of two things happens: either it starts costing more than they're comfortable with, or they finally get a window where they can tackle it without adding stress. Based on what you've said, it sounds like you're in that first camp—it's costing you something, just not enough to jump on yet."

(P) "Is that a fair way to describe it?"

Prospect: "Yeah, that's about right."

"In that case, one simple way we handle it is a short working session where we quantify roughly what it's costing you today and what it would take to fix. No commitment—just clarity. Then you can decide if it earns its way up the priority list or stays where it is."

"Would it be unreasonable to schedule that for, say, next month, when the current fires calm down a bit?"

You didn't push. You didn't argue whether it should be a priority. You helped them think—and offered a next step that matches their world.

What Happens When You Skip SHARP

When You Skip "Stop" (and rush to respond): "Absolutely! I'll send you our full product guide, case studies, pricing overview, implementation timeline, and I'll also include a video walkthrough plus some customer testimonials and..." The prospect checks out. Too much, too fast. You turned a simple request into overwhelm.

When You Skip "Ask" (and assume you know the issue): "I understand, but let me tell you why we're better—our platform has advanced analytics, better integrations, and our customer service is rated number one..." The prospect's walls go up. You're pushing, not listening.

When You Skip "Pack" (and assume agreement): You respond beautifully, then jump straight to: "Great! So let's get something on the calendar for next Tuesday." The prospect says: "Uh, I still need to think about it." You moved forward on an assumption instead of confirmation.

When you use SHARP, the prospect feels heard instead of handled.

That's the difference between pressure and leadership.

AI Assist: Drill SHARP Until Nothing Surprises You

Feed AI your five most common objections and ask it to play a prospect who throws them at you in random order. Run through each one using SHARP—pause, acknowledge, ask one question, respond in under 30 seconds, pack with agreement. After each round, ask: "Which SHARP steps did I hit, which did I skip, and where did I start selling instead of listening?"

For the objections that trip you up most, go deeper. Ask AI: "Play a prospect who says 'we're already working with someone' and push back harder when I ask my clarifying question—don't make it easy." The reps who practice against cooperative simulations build false confidence. The ones who practice against resistance build real composure.

Objections don't get easier with experience. They get easier with reps. AI gives you unlimited reps without burning a single live prospect.

Your Assignment: Day 14 — Practice SHARP Before the Pressure Hits

Here's your challenge for Day 14:

1. List your five most common objections. Write them exactly as your prospects say them.

2. Write one SHARP response for each. Stop (pause). Hear (acknowledgment). Ask (one clarifying question). Respond (20–30 seconds max). Pack (alignment question).

3. Practice out loud and record. Pick two objections. Record yourself handling each with SHARP 5 times. Listen back: Did I actually pause? Did I ask just one question? Did my response stay under 30 seconds?

4. Run a 30-minute call block. When you hear one of the five objections, apply SHARP. After the block, score yourself: Which objection? Did I use SHARP or my old habit? How did the prospect respond?

Because here's the truth most reps never learn:

Indecision is not a threat. It's a signal. A signal that the prospect is still thinking. Still engaged. Still in the conversation.

When you're prepared for that moment—when nothing they say surprises you—you stop fearing objections and start expecting them.

Amateurs panic when objections show up.

Pros expect them—and stay calm when they do.

That's when selling gets simpler. That's when conversations feel calmer. And that's when prospects start trusting you, not because you had all the answers, but because you handled uncertainty better than anyone else they talk to.

Day 14 begins now.

CHAPTER 15

Secure Agreement

Turn Good Calls Into Real Meetings (Or Keep Lying to Yourself)

By now, you've walked through the entire front half of PRECISE:

P — Prepare for the call. **R** — Build Respect and Trust in the first six seconds. **E** — Engage with real questions instead of a product vomit. **C** — Convey a clear, simple reason to keep talking. **I** — Handle Indecision with SHARP instead of panic.

On a good day, a professional rep hits all of those.

And then, in the final sixty seconds of the call, they lose everything.

Not because the product is wrong. Not because the prospect is rude. Not because the objection is impossible.

They lose because they blow the S.

They fail to Secure Agreement.

Most reps don't even know they're doing it. They hang up feeling victorious. They write "Great call!" in their CRM. They tell their manager, "She's really interested."

And two weeks later, they're still waiting for that "interested" person to respond to their email.

Spoiler: she's not going to.

Because interest without a calendar invite is just a polite exit.

The Field Rep Who Did Everything Right... Until He Didn't

Meet Kyle.

Kyle is twenty-nine, sells medical equipment into hospitals and clinics, and is responsible for everything in his territory: Prospecting. Discovery. Closing. The whole thing.

He's no rookie. He's been through the training. He knows the language. He has the PRECISE diagram half-memorized and a laminated version in his car that he pretends he doesn't look at before calls.

On paper, he looks great: Three days a week in the field. Two days in the office. Good with people. Good with questions. Good with stories.

His manager even says, "If Kyle gets in front of the right people, he wins more than his share."

That's the key phrase: "If he gets in front of them."

Because Kyle's problem is not P or R or E or C or I. Kyle's problem is the S.

Tuesday Morning, 9:47 AM

Picture Kyle sitting in his car outside a mid-size hospital, phone on speaker, call notes on the clipboard next to him, coffee getting cold in the cupholder.

He dials the Director of Nursing. He's prepared: he knows her name, her tenure, her likely pressures, and he's seen her LinkedIn post from last week complaining about staffing shortages.

The call goes beautifully:

He builds quick respect and explains why he's calling without sounding like a spam robot. He engages with a couple of sharp, CLEAR-style questions about how they're currently handling a specific problem. He delivers a tight, thirty-second Convey on why a deeper conversation might be worth her time. When she hesitates ("We're already working with someone..."), he uses SHARP, asks one smart question, and uncovers that their current vendor is slow and reactive.

He is doing the job, and it's working.

She's answering. She's opening up. She's even laughing a little.

This is the moment a lot of reps dream about: A live human. The right title. Real pain. Real curiosity. Real engagement.

Everything PRECISE is designed to create is happening.

And then Kyle says:

"Yeah, this has been a great conversation. I'll shoot you some times for a longer meeting and you can just let me know what works."

She says, "Sure, that sounds good."

They hang up.

Kyle leans back in his seat, feeling awesome. He checks the boxes on his notes: "Great call." "Interested." "Said yes to a meeting."

He takes a sip of his now-cold coffee, scrolls his phone for a minute, and feels like he just scored a win.

Except he didn't. He tripped just before the finish line.

What Really Just Happened

Here's what Kyle thinks happened: Built rapport. Created curiosity. Handled objection. Got agreement to meet.

Here's what actually happened: There is no date. There is no time. There is no calendar invite. There is no commitment.

There is just: An inbox full of other people's priorities. Another hundred emails between now and when Kyle "shoots some times." Another seven fires she has to put out today.

Kyle will absolutely write "Follow up with DON — said yes to meeting" on his to-do list. He might draft a beautiful email with three carefully worded time options and a professional signature with his headshot and company logo.

But by the time that shows up in her inbox—if it shows up at all— she barely remembers who he is.

From Kyle's perspective, he secured agreement. From reality's perspective, he secured nothing.

He did PRECI...

He skipped the S.

Assumptions don't show up on calendars. And calendars are the only scoreboard that matters.

A Soft "Yes" Is a Hidden "Maybe"

When a prospect says: "Yeah, send me some times." "Let's connect next week." "I'd definitely like to learn more." "This sounds interesting—let's stay in touch."

They are not saying yes to a meeting.

They are saying things like: "I'm being polite because I don't want confrontation." "I want to end this call without feeling rude." "You seem nice, so I'm not going to hard-reject you." "I'm busy and unsure if this matters."

Interested is not booked.

Interested is the participation trophy of sales.

You don't get credit for "almost." You don't get paid for "pretty sure they'll follow up." Results show up when meetings hit calendars.

Soft language—"I'll send you some times"—is where good conversations go to die.

What Secure Agreement Actually Means

On a prospecting call—or a field pop-in—Secure Agreement does not mean: "They liked me." "They said this is interesting." "They told me to send some times." "They said, 'Let's touch base next week.'" "We had a great conversation."

None of those are wins. Those are opinions.

The win is not emotional. The win is observable. Think of it like a race: you don't get a medal for running hard and stopping two steps before the finish line; you get credit when you cross it.

Secure Agreement means: You asked for a specific next step: a deeper discovery meeting. You offered two concrete options instead of punting to email. You pulled out your calendar while you were still live with them. You sent the invite before you left the lobby or hung up. You stayed with them until they said, "Got it... accepted."

Anything less is a maybe—no matter how good it felt.

The only scoreboard that matters is simple:

Did a deeper discovery meeting land on the calendar before the conversation ended?

Yes = win. No = everything else was warm-up.

If it's not on the calendar, it didn't happen.

The Two Jobs of a Prospecting Call

Prospecting calls—and field pop-ins—have exactly two jobs:

1. Create enough curiosity and safety that a deeper conversation makes sense.

2. Secure agreement to that deeper conversation on a real calendar.

That's it. Not: Teach them everything. Qualify them to death. Pitch the full solution. Close the deal on the first call. Build a "relationship" that goes nowhere.

The last fourteen chapters focused on Job 1. This chapter is about Job 2.

If you nail Job 1 and blow Job 2, you still lose.

The Voice in Your Head That Kills the S

In the final sixty seconds of Kyle's call, he isn't stupid, lazy, or unprepared. He's scared.

The voice in his head sounds like: "Don't push too hard... you don't want to seem desperate." "She already said she's interested... that's good enough." "If I ask for the meeting right now, it might feel pushy." "What if she says no after such a good conversation?"

Every one of those thoughts feels protective. Every one of them is wrecking the pipeline.

Here's the truth: Prospects don't think you're pushy when you ask for a meeting. They think you're professional.

And if they do think you're pushy for calmly asking for 30 minutes? They were never going to buy anyway.

Stop protecting feelings that don't matter.

Start protecting the one thing that does: your pipeline.

Why Soft Language Is Career Cancer

Listen to how average reps end their calls: "I'll send you some times." "Let me know what works for you." "We can connect sometime next week." "I'll shoot you an email."

Every one of those phrases: Pushes the real decision into the future. Hands control back to the prospect's overcrowded inbox. Turns a live yes into a silent maybe.

That isn't prospecting. It's calendar cosplay.

Professionals treat the last minute of the call like the last minute of a game: Clock is running. Ball is in their hands. The play has one purpose: get the meeting.

They use language that assumes movement: "Let's do this..." "Here's what I recommend..." "Let's grab 30 minutes to go deeper on this..."

And then they anchor the S with specifics: Two concrete options. Calendar out. Invite sent and accepted before goodbye.

How Amateurs Lose at the Finish Line

Amateur Move 1: "I'll Send You Some Times" — Rep: "So based on what you shared, it sounds like this could be really helpful." Prospect: "Yeah, definitely worth exploring." Rep: "Great! I'll send you some times and you can let me know what works." Prospect: "Sounds good." What just happened: No date. No time. No urgency. No commitment. Outcome: ghost.

Amateur Move 2: "Just Email Me When You're Free" — Rep: "I think a deeper conversation would make sense." Prospect: "Yeah, probably." Rep: "Perfect. Just shoot me an email when you have some time and we'll get something on the books." The rep just asked a busy prospect—who didn't reach out in the first place—to take initiative and email them later. Outcome: never happens.

Amateur Move 3: "We Should Definitely Connect" — Rep: "We should definitely connect again soon." Prospect: "Absolutely." What just happened: nothing. "Should" is not a commitment. "Soon" is not a date. "Definitely" is conversational filler. Outcome: both people feel good. Neither follows up.

How Professionals Close the Loop

Same moment, handled by a pro:

Rep: "This has been really helpful. Based on what you've shared, the best next step is a short working session where we map this to your specific world and see if there's a real fit."

Prospect: "Yeah, that makes sense."

Rep: "Great. I'm looking at next week—does earlier in the week or later usually work better for you?"

Prospect: "Later is usually better."

Rep: "Perfect. I've got Thursday at 10:15 or Friday at 2:30 open for a 30-minute deep dive. Which is better for you?"

Prospect: "Let's do Thursday at 10:15."

Rep: "Done. I'll send that over right now while we're on the phone. What's the best email for the calendar invite?"

"There it is—should be in your inbox now. Do you mind just making sure it came through and hitting accept so we're both locked in?"

Prospect: "Yep, got it. Accepted."

Rep: "Perfect. See you Thursday at 10:15. Thanks for your time today."

What just happened: A real meeting. On a real calendar. With a real time. With real commitment.

Outcome: the meeting happens.

The difference is not talent. It's discipline.

The S Framework (Five Moves, One Minute)

Use this pattern on every prospecting call or field interaction:

1. Bridge — Acknowledge the conversation and create the transition. "This has been really helpful." "I'm glad we connected today."

2. Recommendation — Tell them what should happen next. "The best next step is a short working session where we map this to your world and see if there's a real fit."

3. Two Options — Offer a simple choice. "I'm looking at next week—does earlier in the week or later usually work better for you?"

4. Calendar Out — Give two specific times while you still have them live. "I've got Tuesday at 10:15 or Thursday at 2:30 open for a 30-minute deep dive. Which is better for you?"

5. Invite Now — Send the calendar invite before you hang up, and get them to accept. "I'll send that over right now while we're on the phone... can you just confirm it came through and click accept so we're both locked in?"

That's Secure Agreement. Clear. Specific. On the calendar before goodbye.

In the Field: Hallway Chaos, Same S

Now picture a field day. You've caught a manager in a hallway between patients or meetings. You introduced yourself without sounding like a stalker, asked one smart question, shared a 20-second Convey.

They say: "Yeah, that's interesting, but I only have a couple minutes right now."

Perfect. You're not trying to do full discovery here. Your entire job is to secure a real meeting when they're not being paged every 19 seconds.

It sounds like this:

"Totally get it—you're in the middle of the chaos here. This deserves more than a two-minute hallway chat. Let's grab 30 minutes when you can actually think."

"I'm back in this area next Wednesday and Friday—what's better for you? Morning or afternoon usually safer?"

"Okay, let's do Friday at 8:45 before things blow up. Does that work? Great, I'll send a calendar invite right now so it doesn't get lost. What's the best email for that?"

"There it is—would you mind just hitting accept so it sticks on both our calendars?"

Same S. Different environment.

What You Don't Say Anymore

Once you start talking like this, some phrases disappear from your vocabulary:

"I'll send you some times." "Just email me when you're free." "We'll connect sometime next week." "I'll shoot you some information and we can go from there."

Those are what average reps say when they're afraid to finish the play.

Calendar cosplay doesn't pay commissions.

Prospects don't need more vague promises. They need a professional who knows what should happen next and is willing to guide them there—calmly, clearly, and with a real time on the calendar.

The Close: Lock This In

You didn't do all that work—preparation, respect, hooks, questions, handling objections—to walk away without asking for the meeting.

You can keep playing calendar cosplay—sending emails into the void, hoping people follow up, lying to yourself about "momentum"—or you can become the professional who finishes the play.

One of those builds a career. The other builds excuses.

Securing agreement isn't pushy. It's professional.

If you don't ask, you didn't prospect. You just had a nice chat.

Nice chats don't pay mortgages.

Nice chats don't hit quota.

Nice chats don't build careers.

Meetings do.

Your Assignment: Day 15 — Finish the Play

Here's your challenge for Day 15:

1. The Last 60 Seconds Only. For ten minutes, rehearse only the final minute of a call. Start at the moment the prospect has shown interest. From there: make a clear recommendation, offer two options, pull out the calendar, send the invite, get them to "accept." Run it over and over until asking for the meeting feels as normal as saying goodbye.

2. One Day, 100 Percent S. Pick one day this week. Give yourself one rule: "I do not end a live conversation without either a real meeting on the calendar, or a conscious, explicit decision not to move forward." No more soft language. At the end of the day, count your real meetings.

3. Audit Your Last Ten Calls. Look at calls where you wrote "Great conversation" or "Very interested." For each one, ask: "Is there a scheduled meeting on the calendar?" Then send three of them a direct follow-up: "We never actually picked a time for that deeper conversation. Let's fix that now—Tuesday at 10 or Thursday at 2. Which is better?"

Because here's the truth most reps never learn:

The best prospecting call in the world is worthless if it doesn't end with a meeting on the calendar.

Amateurs end calls feeling good about "interest." Pros end calls with committed time blocks.

Day 15 begins now.

CHAPTER 16

Explore

Get the Real Decision Makers in the Room (Or Keep Running Great Meetings That Go Nowhere)

Nothing is more soul-crushing than running the best discovery call of your life for the wrong half of the buying team.

You prepare like a maniac, secure the meeting, block the time, maybe even travel across town, and show up ready to go. Then the call starts and it's: you, your slides, your questions, and one very friendly person who "loves what you're saying" but can't sign anything more serious than a birthday card.

You run a killer meeting anyway. You ask great questions, uncover real pain, and map out a powerful future state. They nod, take notes, and say all the magic words: "This is really helpful." "We definitely need something like this." "I can see this making a big impact."

You hang up feeling like you just won a championship.

Then 48 hours later, reality punches you in the throat: "I shared it with my boss, and she has some questions." "We need to loop in finance before we go any further." "IT is going to have concerns about integration." "Our regional director will want to see this."

Translation: you just ran a TED Talk for someone who can't actually say yes.

You didn't explore the decision landscape. You didn't explore who can kill this later if they weren't in the room early. Now, instead of momentum, you have three more meetings to schedule, three more calendars to fight, three more chances for this thing to stall out and die quietly.

Because you skipped the E. You didn't Explore.

The Six-Week Hall Monitor Lesson

Meet Rachel. Three years in, quota-crushing, full pipeline.

She once spent six weeks running "great meetings" with an Operations Director who took perfect notes, loved her solution, and nodded at every ROI slide. Rachel did everything "right": built rapport, asked solid questions, uncovered real pain, delivered a killer demo, mapped out ROI.

The Director said things like: "This is exactly what we need." "I'm going to push hard for this." "Let me get this in front of the team."

Rachel walked out of every meeting feeling like a champion. She wrote "Hot opportunity" in the CRM, told her manager it was a done deal, and started spending the commission in her head.

Six weeks in, she finally asked the question that should have been asked on Day 1:

"Walk me through how this actually gets approved."

And she heard: "I'll present it to the VP. She'll run it by finance. They'll want IT to weigh in. If it's over a certain amount, the regional director has to sign off."

"So... you don't actually approve this?"

"Oh, no. I just research options and make recommendations."

Six weeks of meetings, demos, emails, follow-ups, and "great conversations" with someone who had zero authority to buy. It wasn't the Director's fault. It was Rachel's—because she never asked.

She assumed: engaged = empowered, took the meeting = makes the decision, "we need this" = "I can say yes." She was wrong.

Always explore who's really in the room—before you burn your best material on the wrong audience.

What Explore Really Means Now

Once you've secured a deeper meeting (S), you Explore the buying map. That means you look for: Who lives with the problem every day. Who owns the budget or results. Who worries about risk, compliance, or IT. Who will feel blindsided if they only hear about this after the fact.

Explore is where you stop pretending "my contact" is "the decision maker" just because they're nice to you. Explore is where you make sure the right people are in the room before you burn your best discovery.

Because a great meeting with the wrong room is not a win. It's a very expensive rehearsal.

Why Reps Avoid Explore

Most reps know they should ask "who else needs to be involved." They just don't. Explore feels risky:

Questioning your champion's authority. "If I ask who else is involved, it sounds like I don't trust them."

Making the sale more complicated. "If I bring in more people, there are more chances for someone to say no."

Sounding political or manipulative. "I don't want to look like I'm trying to go around them."

Admitting you don't know what you're doing. "If I have to ask who the decision maker is, I look like a rookie."

Every one of those fears feels protective. Every one of them is destroying your pipeline.

Because if you don't explore who's involved before the meeting, you will absolutely discover who's involved after—in surprise objections from people you've never met, in "we have to pause while we get internal alignment" emails, in ghost mode when your champion gets overruled by someone whose name you still don't know.

Explore isn't risky. Not exploring is what's risky.

The Four People Explore Hunts For

Titles change. Org charts change. But on almost every meaningful deal, the same four roles show up.

In simpler sales, you might find one person per role. In complex enterprise deals, you might find three Operators, two Owners, five Gatekeepers. The roles stay the same. The headcount scales.

If one of them is missing, you're building a wobbly table. Wobbly tables collapse the moment someone leans on them.

1. The Operator — "If This Sucks, I Hear About It." The Operator's life either gets easier or turns into a nightmare depending on whether your solution actually works. They use it every day, train others on it, get blamed if it breaks, get no credit if it succeeds.

Their core question: "Will this make my job harder before it makes it easier?"

Explore language: "Day to day, whose job gets most impacted if this works?" "Who on your team would be using this the most?"

Ignore the Operator and they will quietly resist your solution into oblivion.

2. The Owner — "Whose Budget Is This Coming From?" The Owner signs, approves, or strongly influences the spend—or owns the business result. Sometimes your contact is both Operator and Owner. Often they are not.

In a complex deal, this might be a VP of Operations, a service line leader, or a CFO who never attends the first call but absolutely has an opinion later.

You need to know that before you invest three meetings trying to close someone who can't approve a 50-dollar expense report.

Explore language: "When you've invested in tools like this before, whose budget did it usually come from?" "Who ultimately has to be comfortable with the spend?"

You're not asking, "Can I talk to your boss?" You're asking, "Whose world does this show up in on a P&L or report?"

3. The Gatekeeper — "Who Can Say No Later?" The Gatekeeper doesn't care if your solution cures world hunger. They care about not having to clean up your mess.

They're the person who appears three weeks into a deal and says, "Yeah, this violates our security policy." Suddenly your champion looks at you like you just got them in trouble with the adults.

Gatekeepers care about: risk, compliance, security, legal terms, data, procurement rules. They're not always "Head of IT" or "Legal." Sometimes they're a compliance nurse, a regional ops director, or a procurement analyst with veto power.

Explore language: "On things like this, who usually makes sure it checks the boxes for IT, security, or compliance?" "Who has stopped projects like this in the past because they had concerns?"

You're not dodging the Gatekeeper. You're inviting them in early, when you can still adjust—instead of meeting them for the first time in a rejection email.

4. The Absorber — "Who Gets This Dropped on Their Desk?" The Absorber doesn't own the budget but carries the implementation weight: the team lead who has to roll it out, the admin who has to manage it, the "super user" who trains everyone else.

If they're not part of the conversation, you get: quiet resentment, passive resistance, "We just don't have capacity right now."

Explore language: "If this moves forward, who's likely to have this land on their desk to help roll it out?" "Who usually ends up as the point person when you bring in something new?"

Bringing the Absorber in early avoids drama and gives you an internal ally who cares about practicality.

How to Explore Right After You Secure the Meeting

The best time to Explore decision makers is immediately after you lock in the meeting—not three emails later, not the day before, not when you show up and realize it's just you and the warm-up act.

Step 1: Make It About Protecting Their Time. "To make this worth your time, let's make sure we've got the right people in the room." "I want to avoid you having to repeat this whole conversation to others later." Now Explore feels like a favor you're doing for them—not a favor you're asking.

Step 2: Ask How They've Done This Before. Instead of "Who's the decision maker?", use their own history: "When you've moved forward with something like this before, who usually ends up involved?" "Last time you brought in a new tool or vendor, who had to weigh in?" History is less threatening than hierarchy.

Step 3: Gently Surface the Four Roles. Ask one question aimed at each—spread over 20–40 seconds. Operator: "Day to day, whose job gets most impacted?" Owner: "Whose budget or targets does this tie back to?" Gatekeeper: "Who usually sanity-checks things like this for IT, security, or compliance?" Absorber: "If this moves forward, who ends up being the point person rolling it out?" You're not grilling them. You're helping them think through their own world.

Step 4: Suggest Adding Names, Not Titles. "Would it make sense to include Alex in this first conversation so you're not having to replay everything later? We've already got Thursday at 10:15 blocked. Should we update that invite to include Alex as well?" You're not asking for a brand-new time. You're upgrading the one you just secured.

Step 5: If They Resist, Separate "Now" from "Later." "Got it. Is that more about calendars being tight, or more about wanting to see if this is even worth their time first?" "Totally fair. Let's use this first 30 minutes to see if there's even something here. If there is, can we agree the next step would be to bring Taylor into a short follow-up?" You've still done your job: you explored, you surfaced names, you planted the seed that this is a multi-person decision.

The Rep Who Stopped Losing Deals to "Internal Alignment"

One of our reps, Marcus, used to lose enterprise deals two to three months in with the same phrase: "We need some internal alignment."

He'd been working a healthcare system deal for eight weeks. Perfect discovery with the Director of Clinical Operations. Great technical demo with IT. Solid ROI presentation to the VP of Operations. But he'd done all three separately—different weeks, different calls, different stakeholders hearing different versions of the story.

By the time everyone compared notes, the narrative had morphed. IT thought this was an operations tool. Operations thought IT was leading it. Finance heard "cost savings" from one person and "revenue growth" from another. Nobody had the same story. The deal stalled.

After learning Explore, Marcus changed one thing: the moment he secured a meeting, he'd ask: "When you've brought in tools like this before, who usually ends up involved?"

First call using this approach: the Clinical Operations Director said, "Well, IT always has to sign off. My VP will want to see the ROI. And if it touches patient data, Compliance and Privacy both get involved."

Marcus said: "Got it. Rather than me doing five separate conversations where everyone hears a different version, what if we staged this in two phases? Phase 1: you, IT, and your VP in one discovery call so we're all working from the same baseline. Phase 2: if that makes sense, we bring in Compliance and Privacy for a technical/risk review. Would that save you from having to replay this five different times?"

Director: "Yeah, that actually makes way more sense."

Result: Week 1, discovery with Director, IT Manager, and VP (three people, one story). Week 3, technical/risk review with Compliance and Privacy. Week 5, executive approval with CFO. Deal closed in six weeks instead of dying after three months of "internal alignment" chaos.

Marcus didn't learn a new process. He learned to apply PRECISE Explore at the scale the deal required.

How Amateurs Get Blindsided (And Pros Don't)

Amateur: Rep secures a meeting with the Director of Operations. Runs textbook discovery. Uncovers real pain. Delivers solid demo. Director says, "This is great. Let me run it by the team." Rep writes: "Strong interest. Waiting on internal discussion."

Two weeks later: "I shared this with the CFO and she has concerns about ROI. We're going to hold off." The CFO—who the rep has never met—kills the deal based on a secondhand summary from someone who isn't trained to sell.

Outcome: dead deal, wasted time.

Pro: Rep secures the meeting, then before hanging up says: "To make this worth your time, let's make sure we've got the right people in the room. When you've moved forward with something like this before, who usually ends up involved?" Director: "Well, the CFO will want to weigh in."

Rep: "Would it make sense to include her in this first conversation? We've already got Thursday at 10:15 blocked. Should we update that invite?"

Meeting happens with Director and CFO. CFO hears the ROI story directly. Deal moves forward with both champions aligned.

The difference is not talent. It's Explore.

Stop Selling to Empty Rooms

There are only two kinds of discovery calls:

The ones where you talk to a contact.

The ones where you talk to a buying team.

Contacts are nice. They give good quotes. They nod a lot. Buying teams make decisions.

Explore is the moment you stop pretending those two are the same. It's where you ask how they've done this before. Find out who lives with the problem. Find out who owns the budget. Find out who can stop this later. Find out who will carry the weight.

Then you do the professional thing: you get them in the room—now or in the very next step.

When you combine Secure Agreement (getting the meeting) and Explore (getting the right people into the meeting), you stop running great calls that go nowhere. You start running meetings that can actually move a deal.

Your Assignment: Day 16 — Explore the Room

Here's your challenge for Day 16:

1. The "Who Else" Reps. For ten minutes, practice the 30–60 seconds after you secure a meeting. Protect their time. Ask how they've done this before. Gently surface the four roles. Suggest adding names to the invite. Run it until Explore feels as normal as securing the meeting.

2. The Resistant Champion. Practice with a partner who keeps saying: "Let's just start with me." "My boss is too busy." Stay calm. Separate "now" from "later." At least get agreement on what "later" looks like.

3. Audit Your Pipeline. Look at your current opportunities. For each one, ask: do I know who the Operator, Owner, Gatekeeper, and

Absorber are? If not, your next conversation should include Explore questions.

Because here's the truth most reps never learn:

The best discovery call in the world is worthless if you're talking to someone who can't say yes.

Amateurs run great meetings with the wrong people. Pros make sure the right people are in the room before the meeting starts.

Day 16 begins now.

CHAPTER 17

Warm Calls to Real Deals

Setting the Tone Before the Questions Start

You did the hard part. You prospected. You got hung up on. You got ghosted. You got told, "Just send me something." And through persistence and the frameworks you've learned, you got a meeting on the calendar.

Or sometimes, you didn't have to do any of that. They came to you: "Talk to Sales" form, webinar reply, trade show walk-up.

Either way, you end up in the same place: a warm meeting on your calendar. A real 30–45 minutes where someone has agreed to talk about their world and maybe your solution.

This chapter is about everything that happens before the first question: how you prepare, how you show up, how you look and sound when that meeting starts, and how you transition from pleasantries to game time—cleanly, professionally, and without wasting the first fifteen minutes talking about fishing.

We'll get to the fishing. But first: preparation and professionalism.

Prepare the Same Way Every Time

Before you worry about how to open a warm meeting, lock in what stays the same regardless of how the meeting landed on your calendar: preparation.

1. Review What You Already Know. Pull up CRM notes from the SDR or form fill, the original email, call notes, or trade show notes. Look for: the problem they mentioned, the language they used, what triggered them to reach out or agree to meet. Skip this, and you'll ask questions the SDR already covered.

2. Check Who's Actually in the Meeting. Look at names and titles on the invite. Using your Explore model, ask: Do we have the Operator, Owner, Gatekeeper, Absorber? Note the gaps. You're not canceling if someone's missing; you're just aware of what you're walking into and who you might need next.

3. Set Your Outcomes. Before every warm meeting, decide: minimum outcome = a clear, scheduled next step that involves the right people; ideal outcome = agreement on a problem worth solving plus a concrete path (pilot, evaluation, deeper technical session, or proposal discussion). If you don't decide this before the call, you drift.

4. Build Your Recap Slide (for SDR or Cold-Call Handoffs). For virtual calls where an SDR or prior conversation generated the meeting, build one slide: left side = "What we know so far" (3–5 bullets). Right side = "What we still need to understand" (3–5 bullets). It shows you've listened and gives you an easy way to steer back if things drift.

Preparation is table stakes. Now let's talk about what happens when you walk into the room or click "Join."

Setting the Tone In Person

The meeting starts the second you walk through the door. Not when you open your mouth. Not when you pull up your slides. The second they see you.

Everything about how you carry yourself in the first 30 seconds tells the room whether they're dealing with a professional or a vendor.

If it's four or more people, stand up. This is not optional. When you're presenting to a group—four, six, ten people—you stand. You're leading this meeting, not attending it. Standing communicates authority, energy, and professionalism. It keeps you from slouching into peer mode with the one person you know while ignoring the three you don't. It also gives you natural command of the room—your eye contact improves, your voice projects better, and your body language reads as confident instead of casual. If there's a whiteboard or a screen, own that space.

Dress one level above the room. Not a costume. Not a three-piece suit when everyone's in scrubs. But if the room is business casual, you're in a sport coat. If they're in polos, you're in a button-down. You are asking someone to spend money with you. Look like you take that seriously. When in doubt, overdress. No one ever lost a deal because they looked too professional.

Eye contact with everyone, not just your champion. The biggest mistake reps make in multi-person meetings is spending the entire time looking at the one person they already know. The Owner is watching. The Gatekeeper is watching. The Absorber is watching. If you only talk to your champion, everyone else feels invisible—and invisible people don't advocate for you later.

Own the room setup. If the setup buries you at the far end of the table where half the room can't see you, politely adjust: "Mind if I move down here so I can see everyone?" That's not pushy. That's professional.

You're not a guest. You're the one they made time for.

Setting the Tone on Virtual

Everything that matters in person still matters on a screen. The difference is you have less real estate to prove it—and more ways to blow it.

Branded or clean professional background. Not your messy apartment. Not a fake beach. Not a bookshelf designed to make you look intellectual. A clean background with your company logo or a simple, professional setup. The prospect's first impression on Zoom is your background before you say a word. Make it look like you do this for a living.

Head centered in the camera. Not cut off at the forehead. Not shot from below like a hostage video. Not six feet away so you're a tiny figure in a giant room. Your head should be in the upper third of the frame, centered, with a little space above. Look at your preview before every call. This takes three seconds and most reps never do it.

Good lighting. Face lit, not backlit into a silhouette. If you're sitting in front of a window, you're a shadow. If you're in a dark room, you look like you're hiding. A simple ring light or desk lamp aimed at your face fixes this. Prospects can't trust what they can't see.

Dress professionally. Nothing drives me more nuts than a software rep who thinks it's cool to have his hat on backwards, talking like a cocky SaaS bro who just rolled out of bed. You are asking a human being to spend real money—maybe tens or hundreds of thousands of dollars—based partly on whether they trust you. The backwards hat, the hoodie, the "we're a startup, we're casual" uniform—that's not confidence. That's laziness dressed up as culture. Dress like you respect their time and their money. Period.

Camera on, always. If they have theirs off, you still have yours on. You're the one who asked for this meeting—or the one they're trusting with their time. Showing your face is the baseline of professionalism. If you can't be bothered to turn your camera on, don't be surprised when they can't be bothered to show up to the next call.

Close the extra tabs and notifications. Nothing kills presence like your eyes darting to Slack every ten seconds. Silent black boxes are still part of the buying team. Know who's on and who's off camera before you start.

Virtual meetings are not a lower standard. They're the same standard with a smaller frame. Act accordingly.

The Rep Who Lost a Deal Over a Fish

Now let's talk about what happens when you look the part, you've prepared, and you still blow the first fifteen minutes.

Meet Tyler. Two years in, good numbers, solid product knowledge, genuinely likable.

Tyler walks into a 30-minute meeting with a Director of Operations at a mid-size manufacturing company. There's a mounted largemouth bass on the wall behind the Director's desk.

Tyler's eyes light up.

"Oh man, is that a largemouth? Where'd you catch that?"

The Director smiles. "Lake of the Ozarks. Caught it two summers ago."

"No way. I fish the Ozarks every July. What were you using?"

And they're off. Tyler and the Director spend the next twelve minutes talking about fishing spots, lure selection, boat motors, and a buddy's lake house. It's genuine. It's fun. The Director is laughing.

Tyler is having the time of his life.

Then he looks at his phone. Eighteen minutes left.

He scrambles. He rushes through his opener. He speed-reads his discovery questions. He talks fast, skips the playbacks, glosses over the Director's answers. He gets to his Convey and it sounds like an auctioneer trying to close before the gavel drops.

The Director says, "Yeah, this sounds interesting. Send me something."

Tyler drives back to the office feeling great. "We really connected. He loves fishing. We bonded."

The Director never responds to the follow-up email.

Tyler blames timing. Tyler blames budget. Tyler blames the economy.

The real reason? Tyler spent 40 percent of a 30-minute meeting talking about a fish. He never got to the Director's real problems. He never went vertical on anything that mattered. He never built the kind of trust that comes from understanding someone's business—not their hobbies.

The Director liked Tyler. He just didn't respect him enough to give him a second meeting.

Likable is not professional. Small talk is not selling. And bonding over a fish is not building trust.

Pleasantries: 60 to 90 Seconds, Then the Whistle Blows

To be clear: small talk is not forbidden. It's human. Ignoring the bass on the wall would be weird. Asking about their weekend when they mention it is fine. Acknowledging you saw their LinkedIn post about a team milestone is a nice touch.

But you control the clock. Not the conversation.

Sixty to ninety seconds of pleasantries. That's it. Enough to be human. Not enough to lose the meeting.

Then the whistle blows. Game time. And game time starts with the Warm Open.

The Warm Open: Thank → Context → Path

Whether they came to you or you earned this meeting through a cold call, you need a clean, repeatable warm open. No winging it. No sliding into a demo. No rambling through five minutes of throat-clearing before anyone knows why they're here.

The structure is simple: **Thank → Context → Path.**

Thank = Appreciate their time and lower their defenses.

Context = Briefly connect to what you already know.

Path = Set a simple agenda and check it with them.

Used well, this takes 20–40 seconds. Let's start with the Thank—because it's not a throwaway line. It's a precision tool.

Thank

The PRECISE Warm Opener:

"Thank you for your time today. I know your time is important, so I'd like to make our visit together as quick and as valuable as possible. I can do this by asking you a couple of quick questions. If you believe that we might have a solution for you, then we can discuss it in further detail. If not, I thank you for the opportunity."

Every word earns its spot:

"Thank you for your time." Most reps don't even bother to thank prospects for giving them the opportunity to speak. They act like it's their God-given right to be in front of customers, when customers are doing them a favor by taking time out of their busy day. When you open with these two words, you immediately set yourself apart from the average salesperson. They break down the wall of apprehension that most customers bring into a sales call.

"I know your time is important." What do most customers think a sales rep is going to do during a scheduled appointment? Waste time by talking too much. Because you know that's what they're thinking, you disarm them by bringing up the time concern before they do. You put their minds at ease.

"Quick and valuable." Most customers are skeptics. They think most of what you're going to say will have little value to them. When you tell them your intentions are to save them time and make every word valuable, the reaction is relief. And when the customer is relieved, your chances of getting your message across are greatly improved.

"Quick questions." The word "quick" appears twice—by design. You want them to know you plan to do your job effectively in the shortest time possible. When they realize your questions are the vehicle that helps you save their time, they're much less apprehensive about letting you question them. In fact, they become eager to share information because they understand it's in their best interest.

"If you believe." These three words let customers know they are in control and that the buying decisions are theirs alone. Letting them know up front that their opinions and beliefs supersede yours blows a big hole through the defenses.

"Might have a solution. If not, thank you." This insinuates that you, as the salesperson, are not even sure if what you have is going to provide a solution to their needs. It lets them know you have no plans to pressure them and removes yet another brick in the defense wall.

The typical response? While their faces usually say, "Whew, amen, thank goodness this is not another sales schmuck," their lips usually say one of two things:

"Thank you for coming. Feel free to ask questions. Oh, and by the way, I am not in a hurry, so take your time."

"Thanks for coming. I appreciate your concern for my time, and I do only have seven minutes to chat."

Either response gives you valuable information. Now you know exactly how much time you have—and you got that information softly, without awkwardly asking, "How much time do we have today?"

Context

Right after the opener, connect to what you already know. One or two sentences. You're proving you listened, not starting from zero.

"From what I captured in our initial conversation, it sounds like [problem in their words]."

Or if they came to you:

"From what I've seen so far, it looks like you're looking at [what they expressed interest in]."

If an SDR generated the meeting and you're on Zoom, this is where you pull up the recap slide: "On the left here is what we heard from you so far—does that look directionally right? On the right are some of the areas we'd love to understand better today."

Let them edit you. "We actually don't use that system anymore." "It's not so much the volume; it's the variability." Every correction they make deepens trust—because you invited it.

Path

Give the meeting a simple destination and check it with them.

"My goal for this call is to confirm if that's really the problem, understand how it's showing up today, and, if it makes sense, outline what a next step with your team could look like. Does that match what you were hoping to cover, or is there anything else you want to make sure we hit?"

That last question is critical. It invites them to shape the meeting instead of just sitting through yours. When they say "Yes, that's right" or adjust the agenda, you've aligned the meeting with what matters to them—not what your slide deck assumes matters.

Use the same Thank → Context → Path structure on every warm meeting. In person and on Zoom. Whether they came to you or you cold-called your way to the calendar invite. Consistency is what makes you sound like a pro instead of someone improvising through the first five minutes.

The Bridge Into Engage

After the Warm Open, how you move into questions depends on how the meeting got on your calendar.

If a cold call, SDR, or outbound effort generated the meeting: Your Context and recap slide already set the table. From here, go deeper on whatever they confirmed or corrected. You're in Engage.

If they came to you (inbound, form fill, trade show): Start with two trigger questions that set the tone for everything that follows.

Question 1: "What got you interested in wanting to learn more?"

You're looking for the trigger—the moment it shifted from "background annoyance" to "I should talk to someone about this."

Question 2: "Have you already decided there's a need for a solution like this, or are you still deciding if you need to change anything at all?"

You're not asking, "Are you ready to buy?" You're asking, "Are we solving a decided problem or a maybe problem?" Those two answers tell you how urgent this is, whether it's an active project or early exploration, and how hard you'll have to work later.

Either way, you're now in Engage territory—which is exactly where the next chapter picks up.

Your Assignment: Day 17 — Set the Tone Like a Pro

Here's your challenge for Day 17:

1. Audit Your Virtual Setup. Before your next call, check your background, lighting, camera position, and what you're wearing. Take a screenshot of your preview. Would you trust this person with a major purchase? If not, fix it.

2. Practice the Warm Open. For ten minutes, rehearse Thank → Context → Path out loud. Start with the PRECISE opener, bridge into a context statement and path for a real upcoming meeting. Run it until the whole sequence—60 to 90 seconds of pleasantries, then straight into the opener—feels natural, not abrupt.

3. Stand Up on Your Next In-Person Group Meeting. If you're meeting with four or more people, stand. Notice how the energy in the room changes. Notice how your own confidence shifts. Notice how they look at you differently.

4. Time Your Pleasantries. On your next three warm meetings, quietly note when you start and when you deliver the opener. If more than 90 seconds pass between "Hello" and "Thank you for your time," you waited too long. Tighten it up.

Because here's the truth most reps miss:

The first five minutes of a warm meeting don't just set the tone.

They decide whether the rest of PRECISE gets a chance to work.

Amateurs show up unprepared, underdressed, and spend the first fifteen minutes talking about fishing. Pros prepare like professionals, look like professionals, and transition to game time before the prospect wonders why they took this meeting.

Day 17 begins now.

CHAPTER 18

Engage the Warm

How to Question Without Turning Discovery Into an Interrogation

Why Good Questions Asked Badly Still Fail

Let me tell you about the time I ran what I thought was the best discovery of my life—and everyone in the room hated it.

Early in my career, I finally landed a meeting with a hospital system I'd been chasing for months. Six people showed up: Director of Nursing, CFO, two department heads, IT Manager, and the VP of Operations.

I walked in with my leather portfolio, my question list, and what I thought was unshakeable confidence.

And then I did this: "Tell me about your role." "What are your biggest challenges right now?" "How does that impact the business?" "Walk me through your current process." "What happens if you don't fix this?" "Who else is involved in decisions like this?"

On paper, every one of those questions was solid.

In reality? I sounded like an over-caffeinated detective reading off a checklist. No one could finish a thought before I pounced on the next question. One person did 80% of the talking while everyone else silently stared at their notepads or checked their watches.

By the end, I had three pages of notes and exactly zero real connection with anyone in the room.

The feedback from my manager was brutal and fair:

"You asked good questions. You just asked them badly."

That's what this chapter is about. You don't need a giant new list of questions. You need a better way to use the ones you already have—inside a real, warm, often multi-person meeting.

That's Engage, for real.

You Already Know Engage

Earlier in this sprint, you learned E = Engage. You used CLEAR questions to turn cold calls into real conversations. You stopped asking "Do you have any challenges?" and started asking "When was the last time X happened?"

You moved from vague to specific, from hypothetical to concrete. You learned that CLEAR questions are: Specific, not fluffy. Grounded in the prospect's world, not your pitch. Designed to move the conversation one step at a time—not five.

That was Engage in prospecting mode. Now you're in a different arena: This is not a 7-minute cold call. This is a 30–45 minute warm discovery. Sometimes it's just you and one person. Often it's you and three, four, or six people—all with different roles and agendas.

The mistake most reps make? They take the same list of "good questions" and simply stretch it. They ask more of them. Faster. To more people. And suddenly, what should feel like a conversation feels like a deposition.

So you're not going to learn a brand-new Engage. You're going to learn how to use the same Engage inside a room—with inbound context, or SDR notes and a recap slide, and multiple humans staring back at you.

Without making them feel like suspects.

The Warm Rhythm: Question → Reflect → Pivot

The difference between discovery and interrogation isn't the questions—it's the rhythm.

You're going to use a simple cadence in warm meetings:

Question → Reflect → Pivot

Question: Ask one clear, purposeful question (often CLEAR-style).

Reflect: Play back what you heard in a sentence or two; show you actually listened.

Pivot: Decide whether to go deeper on this thread or move to the next logical area.

Most reps skip Reflect and Pivot. They fire Question → Question → Question until everyone wants out.

Here's what that looks like.

Bad rhythm (interrogation)

> *Rep:* "What are your biggest challenges right now?"
>
> *Prospect:* "Honestly, visibility. We don't know what's stuck until a customer yells."
>
> *Rep:* "Got it. And how does that impact the business?"
>
> *Prospect:* "Well, obviously delays, a lot of fire drills."
>
> *Rep:* "Okay. And what happens if you don't fix this?"

It's not that the questions are terrible. It's that there's no reflection and no pivot, just a checklist.

Good rhythm using Question → Reflect → Pivot

> *Rep:* "When jobs get delayed today, what usually causes it?" (Question)
>
> *Prospect:* "Honestly, visibility. We don't know what's stuck until a customer yells."
>
> *Rep:* "So most of the time you're finding out about problems from the customer, not your own system—that's when everyone scrambles?" (Reflect)
>
> *Prospect:* "Exactly. We're always reacting."

Rep: "Got it. That's helpful. From there, where does it hurt most—customer satisfaction, staff burnout, or missed revenue?" (Pivot)

Same basic intent. Same "good" questions. But the Reflect step slows you down, proves you heard them, and earns the right to Pivot without feeling like you're just mining them for data.

Use Question → Reflect → Pivot as the metronome for your warm discovery. Any time you catch yourself stacking questions with no reflection, you're drifting back into interrogation mode.

Why Reps Turn Discovery Into an Interrogation

Most reps don't want to sound like detectives. They don't wake up thinking, "Today I'm going to machine-gun questions at people until they hate me." But they do it anyway.

Why? Because discovery feels like the moment where everything is on the line. You've worked so hard to get this meeting. You've got the right people in the room. You've opened well. And now your brain says: "Don't blow it. Ask everything. Cover all the bases. Qualify thoroughly. Get the information you need."

So reps default to interrogation mode:

They're nervous and cling to their question list. When adrenaline kicks in, the brain reaches for what feels safe—the list of questions you practiced. So you read them. One after another. Without thinking about whether the person just answered three of them in their last response.

They think 'more questions = better discovery.' Most training says: "Make sure you understand the problem, the impact, the budget, the timeline, the decision-making process..." Reps hear that as: "Ask more. Cover everything." So they ask 20. Then 25. Then 30. They think they're being thorough. What they don't realize: the prospect stopped caring around question 7.

They're afraid of silence. After a prospect finishes answering, there's a gap. A moment where nothing is happening. Most reps panic. So they fill that silence immediately with the next question. They don't give the prospect time to think. They don't give themselves time to process what was just said. They just keep moving.

They're worried about losing control. If the prospect starts telling a long story, or goes off on a tangent, reps think: "I'm losing control. I need to get us back on track." So they interrupt. They redirect. They jump to the next question. And what they don't realize is: the tangent was where the truth lived.

Every one of these instincts feels protective. Every one is destroying trust in real time.

Prospects don't want to be qualified. They want to be understood.

And understanding doesn't come from 30 rapid-fire questions. It comes from 5 good questions, asked well, with room to breathe.

CLEAR Questions in a Live Meeting

By the time Engage starts in a warm meeting, you're not starting from zero. You've already opened correctly. You've set expectations. You've either asked your two inbound questions ("What got you interested?" and "Have you decided you need a solution?") or recapped what the SDR learned with your "What we know / What we need to understand" slide.

Now it's time to go deeper. The temptation is to think: "Okay, time to go down my 25 discovery questions." Resist that.

Instead, think of Engage in a warm meeting as: Start from what you already know. Pick one problem that matters. Go vertical, not horizontal.

Horizontal vs. Vertical Discovery

Here's the difference between interrogation and conversation.

Horizontal Discovery sounds like this: "What's your role?" "What are your challenges?" "What tools are you using?" "What's your budget?" "What's your timeline?" You skim across the surface of ten topics and go deep on none. By the end, you have notes on everything and understanding of nothing.

Vertical Discovery sounds like this: "Last time you mentioned that onboarding new reps is taking 90 days instead of 60. When did that start to become a problem?" "How often does it create real issues in a given month?" "What happens on the floor when a new rep isn't fully ready yet?" "How do you feel that in numbers—missed targets, errors, customer complaints?" "Who feels that pain the most?"

Same number of questions. Very different depth.

Whether you're running one discovery call or staging discovery across multiple stakeholder levels, the principle stays the same: go vertical, not horizontal.

In enterprise deals, you'll often run discovery multiple times—once with end users (Operators), again with department heads (mid-level Owners), again with executives (C-suite Owners), and possibly again with risk or compliance teams (Gatekeepers). CLEAR questions work at every level. Same framework, different altitude. You ask "Currently, how often does X happen?" to the ICU nurse manager. You ask "Currently, how does X show up in your operational reports?" to the CFO. The structure doesn't change. The depth and business impact shift based on who you're asking.

Five vertical questions on one real problem will teach you more than twenty horizontal questions about everything they might be struggling with.

Depth beats breadth. Every single time.

How Amateurs Interrogate (And How Professionals Converse)

Amateur Move: Horizontal Discovery Across Five People.
Five people on the call: Director of Ops, CFO, IT Manager, Training Lead, and Regional VP. Rep goes around the room: "What's your

role?" "What are your biggest challenges?" "How does that impact the business?" Asks the same basic questions to each person. By person #3, everyone is mentally checked out. By person #5, two people have their cameras off.

What the prospects are thinking: "Why am I on this call if they're asking me the same questions they asked everyone else?" "I've got three other meetings today. This feels like a waste of time."

Outcome: Lots of notes. Zero connection. No clear problem to solve. Surface-level answers from everyone, deep understanding of no one.

Professional Move: Vertical Discovery on One Real Problem. Same five people. Rep has already recapped what the SDR learned. Rep picks one problem mentioned in the recap: "Last time we talked, you mentioned that onboarding new reps is taking 90 days instead of 60. Let's go a little deeper on that."

Asks the Training Lead (Operator): "When did that start becoming a problem for your team?" Training Lead explains.

Rep does a playback: "So if I'm hearing this right, the shift to remote work added complexity, and now new reps are hitting quota 30 days later than they used to. Is that fair?" Training Lead confirms.

Rep uses a pile-on to bring in the CFO (Owner): "From a finance perspective, how does that 30-day delay show up on your reports?" CFO explains the revenue gap.

Rep uses another pile-on to bring in the IT Manager (Gatekeeper): "From an IT standpoint, is there anything about the current tools making this harder than it needs to be?" IT Manager shares concerns about integration.

Rep tells a short parallel story: "We've seen something similar with a regional bank we work with. They were seeing longer ramp times after going remote, and the real issue ended up being that training content wasn't mobile-friendly, so new reps were trying to learn on laptops in coffee shops instead of on their phones between calls. As you hear that, what feels similar or different about your situation?" Training Lead and Regional VP both respond.

What the prospects are thinking: "This person is actually listening." "They're connecting the dots between what we're all saying." "This feels like a real conversation, not a questionnaire."

Outcome: Deep understanding of one real problem. Multiple people engaged. Clear pain identified. Trust built.

The amateur asked more questions. The professional asked better ones.

CLEAR Questions by Role

In Chapter 16, you met the four people you're exploring for: Operator, Owner, Gatekeeper, Absorber. In a live discovery, Engage means using CLEAR questions that speak to each of these realities. You don't need a new framework. You just need to aim your questions at where people actually live—not where your pitch deck wants them to live.

For the Operator (cares about effort, disruption, "Will this make my life easier or harder?"): "Walk me through the last time this problem showed up for your team. What happened that day?" "On a typical week, how often does this get in the way of you doing your actual job?" "If nothing changed here for the next 6–12 months, what would that mean for your team?"

For the Owner (cares about numbers, outcomes, trade-offs): "When this shows up on your reports, how does it change what you do that week or month?" "If this were solved, which numbers would you expect to see move first?" "If you had to defend this decision internally, what result would you point to 6–12 months from now?"

For the Gatekeeper (cares about risk, compliance, not cleaning up messes): "From a risk or compliance standpoint, what would make this kind of change feel unsafe to you?" "What boxes have to be checked before anything like this can go live here?" "Have you seen projects like this get stopped before? What were the reasons?"

For the Absorber (cares about capacity, practicality, "Is this going to be another thing I'm blamed for?"): "If this landed on your desk to roll out, what would you worry about first?" "What's made similar projects painful here in the past?" "When new tools or processes come in, what usually goes well... and what usually goes sideways?"

You don't need to ask all of these. You do need to make sure each role gets at least one CLEAR question aimed at their world.

Four Tools That Keep Engage from Turning Into Interrogation

Tool 1: Playbacks. A short summary of what you heard, in your own words, followed by a check: "So what you're saying is ____, and that matters because ____. Did I get that right?" Playbacks prove you're listening, give them a chance to correct or deepen what they said, and slow you down. Simple rule: After any meaningful answer, do a playback before you ask your next question.

Tool 2: Pile-Ons. In a multi-person meeting, a pile-on brings others into the conversation without starting from scratch. You take one person's answer and invite others to respond: "That's really helpful from the ops side. How does that land from your perspective in finance?" Pile-ons keep the conversation anchored to one thread and get more people talking without creating whiplash.

Tool 3: Short Parallel Stories. A 20–30 second example that says: "We've seen this before. You're not crazy. There's a path through it." Then pivot back: "As you hear that, what feels similar or different about your situation?" Done right, parallel stories build credibility, make people more comfortable being honest, and open up new angles without you having to grill them. Key rule: Tell the story briefly, then turn it back into a question. Don't make it about you. Make it about them.

Tool 4: Talk Time Awareness. On interrogations, reps often talk 50–60% of the time. On great discovery calls? 30–40%. The math is brutal and honest: If you're doing more talking than listening, you're doing it wrong. No one joins a call thinking: "I really hope this person talks for 60% of the time and asks me 25 questions." Set a simple target: You talk meaningfully less than they do. You ask a question. You shut up. You let silence do some work. You listen.

Make This Style of Engage Automatic

As with everything else in PRECISE, you don't want Engage to depend on "remembering" in the moment.

You want your mouth to feel weird if you're: Machine-gunning through questions without playbacks. Ignoring half the room. Talking more than everyone else combined.

Here's how to build the reflex.

Your Assignment: Day 18 — Ask Better Questions, Not More Questions

Drill 1: Interrogation vs. Conversation. Pick 6 CLEAR questions you actually use. Run two short roleplays. Round 1 (Interrogation): Ask all 6 as fast as you can, no playbacks, no pile-ons. Notice how it feels. Round 2 (Conversation): Same 6 questions, but after every answer do a playback, use at least one pile-on, use one 20–30 second parallel story, leave 2–3 seconds of silence after big answers. You'll feel the difference immediately. Same questions. Completely different experience.

Drill 2: Four Role Round. Set up a 15-minute roleplay. One person plays all four roles: Operator, Owner, Gatekeeper, Absorber. Your job: Ask at least one CLEAR question tailored to each role. Use at least one playback per role. Use at least one pile-on. Afterwards, ask: "Did each role feel seen, or did anyone feel ignored?" "Where did I slip into interrogation mode?"

Drill 3: Talk Time Audit. Record a real discovery meeting. After the call, estimate how much you talked vs. how much they talked. Count your playbacks and pile-ons. On your next three discoveries, aim to lower your talk time and increase your playbacks. You're not chasing perfection. You're making Engage as a conversation your default—not Engage as an interrogation.

It's Still the Same E

Here's the through line:

In prospecting, Engage was how you turned strangers into conversations.

In warm calls, Engage is how you turn meetings into truth.

In multi-person discovery, Engage is how you turn a room of titles into a room of humans you actually understand.

Nothing about the letter changed. You just learned how to use it where it matters most.

Because here's the truth most reps never learn:

The best questions in the world are worthless if you ask them like a detective reading from a checklist.

Amateurs ask more questions and wonder why prospects check out. Pros ask fewer questions, go deeper, and actually listen—and prospects lean in.

Day 18 begins now.

CHAPTER 19

Convey the Solution

How to Turn Bullets Into a Presentation They Can't Walk Away From

Why Reps Turn Convey Into a Feature Parade

Most reps don't want to drown people in features. They don't wake up thinking, "Today I'm going to show 47 tabs and lose everyone by minute 12." But they do it anyway.

Why? Because Convey feels like the moment where you finally get to prove your solution works. You've earned the meeting. You've asked great questions. You've uncovered real pain. And now your brain says: "Don't blow it. Show them everything. Prove you know your product. Make sure they see all the value."

So reps default to feature parade mode:

They're proud of their product. When you believe in what you sell, you want people to see all of it. Every feature. Every integration. What you don't realize: the prospect stopped processing at feature four. By feature twelve, they're mentally gone. By feature eighteen, they're rehearsing their polite exit line.

They think 'more features = more value.' Most product training says, "Here's everything the platform does. Make sure you cover it all." You hear that as, "I need to show everything." But covering everything isn't the job. Making them understand how it helps is the job.

They confuse 'professional' with 'emotionless.' Somewhere along the line, you got the message that enthusiasm is unprofessional. So you flatten your voice. You remove the energy. You hide behind slides. And the prospect checks email. Nobody gets excited about something the presenter doesn't seem to care about.

They're afraid of silence. After you show something, there's a gap—a moment where the prospect might be thinking. Most reps panic. Instead of letting silence breathe, they fill it. "Oh, and let me also show you..." You think you're being thorough. You're actually burying the point you just made.

Prospects don't need to see everything. They need to see what matters to them.

And what matters to them is sitting right in front of you—on your notepad.

Be a Smart Bomb, Not a Dumb Bomb

Large bombers have been a staple in the American military since World War II. Turn on the History Channel and you'll see old footage of B-52s dropping "dumb bomb" after "dumb bomb" over the skies of Germany, Japan, and Vietnam. Carpet bombing was the only way to ensure the mission was accomplished. But there was massive collateral damage in the process.

In modern military times, there are weapons known as smart bombs. The goal of a smart bomb is to engage the target, use only enough ordnance as needed, and be as precise as possible to carry out the mission. They hit more targets with less weapons.

In sales, you too need to be a smart bomb. While your competition is dropping masses of dumb bombs in the form of statements about features, bells, and whistles, you can operate as a precision-guided weapon. By focusing your presentation only on the bullets you uncovered during Engage, your customer will hang on your every word.

Because everything you say is about them. Not about your product. About *their* problems, *their* words, *their* world.

The dumb bomb rep walks in with 47 features and hopes three of them land. The smart bomb rep walks in with three to six bullets and makes every one of them count.

The Transition from Engage to Convey

You've just finished Engage. You've gone vertical on their real problems. You've done playbacks, pile-ons, and parallel stories. You've listened more than you talked. And now you have a notepad with three to six bullets—short phrases, in their words, capturing the problems, goals, and risks they shared with you.

Now it's time to move from questions to presentation. This moment needs a clean, rehearsed transition—not a stumble into "Okay, let me show you what we can do."

Here's the transition I've used for over twenty years:

"Based on what you told me about [bullet A], [bullet B], and [bullet C], I believe we can provide some solutions to some of the challenges you're having. In addition, I think we can even improve on some of the things that are already working well for you. Before we get into a specific discussion about how we might solve some of your current issues, I'd love to tell you a little about our company."

Read that again. Play customer for a moment. How would you feel if a sales rep took the time to question you about your wants and needs, actually listened to what you were saying, and then confidently suggested they have a solution to your problems—without asking you to sacrifice the things that are already working?

The answer I most often get in my seminars is one word: *curious.*

Curious to see if the rep's product can really do what they just said it could. And when a prospect is curious, they're seeking—not defending. The walls of resistance come down. The customer becomes more engaged.

When prospects want, they are more willing to give. And the more willing they are to give, the more able you are to be PRECISE and deliver the perfect solution.

Practice this transition like an actor practices lines. Say it smoothly and with confidence. It should feel as natural as your warm opener.

Notice where the transition lands: not at "Let's take a look." It lands at "I'd love to tell you a little about our company." That's intentional. Because before you go narrow on their bullets, you need to go wide—just for thirty seconds.

Tell Them Who You Are—And Why It Matters More Than You Think

This is the moment where you stick your chest out and show a little pride in who you're representing today.

Most reps skip this step entirely. They hear the prospect's pain during Engage and they can't wait to jump straight to the prescription. "You said onboarding is too slow? Let me show you exactly how we fix that."

That's jumping to the prescription too early. And it's a mistake, because it shrinks you.

When you skip the company pitch and go straight to a single bullet, you become a one-trick pony in the prospect's mind. They think you do one thing. They don't see the full picture. And when they don't see the full picture, they can't imagine all the ways you might help—which means smaller deals, shorter relationships, and no expansion.

Here's the fix. After your transition and before you hit your first bullet, deliver your 30-second elevator pitch—the same one you built in Chapter 13. But now it has a strategic purpose beyond credibility: **it opens their mind to additional ways you can help.**

Let me show you what I mean.

Take PRECISE Selling as an example. Let's say my closer runs a discovery call with a VP of Sales, and the VP's biggest pain point is that his team can't prospect. That's the hot bullet. The temptation is to jump straight into our prospecting training program and show him how we fix it.

But if my closer first takes thirty seconds to tell the VP who we are—that we provide a complete sales operating system including a customized Playbook, a Performers platform for tracking and coaching, AI-powered tools for real-time call support, and marketing services to drive pipeline—something important happens.

The VP's eyes get wider.

He walked into this meeting thinking he needed help with prospecting. Now he's realizing he might need a whole system. We just went from being a sales training company to a sales operating system—all in thirty seconds. And we haven't even started presenting bullets yet.

That's why the elevator pitch lives here, between the transition and the bullets. It's not ego. It's strategy.

Now, of course, you will not make the mistake so many reps make: pulling up six slides on the history of the company and how the founders walked to school uphill both ways. Nobody cares. Two or three sentences. Practiced and polished. Show pride in who you represent, paint a quick picture of the full scope of what you do, and move on.

If what you're saying doesn't help you gain credibility, respect, trust, or expand their view of how you can help—save it.

Your Bullets Are Your Presentation

Here is the most important concept in this chapter, and possibly in this entire book:

Your bullets from Engage are your presentation outline.

During Engage, you captured three to six specific problems, goals, or risks—in their words, not yours. Those short phrases on your notepad are the secret combination to unlock the mind and heart of your prospect.

Your notepad might look like this:

- 3-day service delays

- Reps onboarding too slowly

- No visibility into stuck orders

- Manual reporting eating 10 hrs/week

If a point is not on your bullet list, it does not belong in this presentation.

That's what makes you a smart bomb. You don't carpet bomb with features. You don't open your slide deck and go page by page. You look at your bullets, pick the hottest one, and start there.

Load the Hot Bullet First

Your next step is to hit your bullets. Grab your notepad and start from the hot bullet—the one you believe will have the most immediate impact.

This is the bullet that carries the most pain or the biggest payoff. Maybe the prospect told you they're wasting ten hours a week on manual reporting. Maybe their onboarding process is costing them a month of lost productivity per new hire. Maybe their service delays are driving customers to competitors.

Whichever bullet made the room go quiet during Engage— whichever one got the longest answer, the most head-nodding, the most emotion—that's your hot bullet. Start there.

You want the most bang for your buck immediately. Start with the bullet that carries the most interest, and you'll have their attention for everything that follows.

Each Bullet Gets Its Own Presentation

This is the core of Convey, and this is where most reps get it wrong.

Most salespeople—if they've even gotten this far in the sales process—roll all their bullets into one large presentation. They lump everything together into a thirty-minute feature tour and hope something sticks.

The PRECISE sales rep does it differently. You attack each bullet separately. You open a discussion on that one topic, explain why your solution addresses it, and get an agreement on that bullet before moving to the next.

Here is the rhythm for each bullet:

1. Re-state the bullet in their words. "You told me the big issue is that approvals get stuck and can take up to three days." This proves you listened. It also brings the pain back to the surface.

2. Ask a Consequence Question to make them feel it again. "What happens downstream when approvals take that long?" "Where does that show up for your team?" These questions turn a hot bullet into a white-hot bullet. It is not enough to know someone has a problem. You need to find out the consequences of that problem while getting them to feel the pain all over again. This is where you make the most impact in your presentation.

3. Show the benefit first, then the minimum feature. Lead with what your solution does for them, not what your solution is. "This is where we help. Our customers use [solution] so they can see every approval status in one place and clear bottlenecks in minutes instead of days." The benefit is the relief. The feature is the mechanism. Benefits first, features second—always.

4. Ask them to sell it to themselves. "Based on what I just shared, where might that help you in your world?" "Where do you see that making the biggest difference for your team?" This is huge. Instead of you dumping more content, you force them to translate your solution into their reality. They start describing their own processes, their own bottlenecks, their own moments in the day. They're now doing the selling.

5. Get a little yes. "Does that line up with what you're dealing with?" "Can you see how that would give you some of that time back?"

6. Check off the bullet. Physically. Draw a line through it on your notepad. Grey it out on your slide. Add a check mark. Let them see you do it. It's visual, it's tactile, and it communicates: that topic is handled. We're making progress. Then—and only then—you move to the next bullet.

You do not mash all four or five bullets into one giant speech. Each bullet gets its own mini-presentation and its own little agreement.

A Bunch of Little Yeses Become One Big Yes

Every time you run that bullet rhythm, a few important things happen:

Little yes: they nod when you re-state the bullet in their words.

Little yes: they agree the consequence is painful. "Yeah, that's killing us."

Little yes: they say "that would help" after you show the benefit.

Little yes: they give you their own example of where it helps.

Little yes: they agree with your check-in question. "Yeah, that makes sense."

By the time you get to the end of the conversation, you don't need a magic closing line. You've already built one.

A bunch of little yeses become one big yes.

Benefits First, Features Second

Salespeople love features. Buyers love what features do for them.

Most reps have no problem discussing features. Features are easy to find on a brochure, easy to remember, and easy to spew. Changing salespeople from B-52 feature bombers to precision benefit-dropping machines is not easy. It takes a fundamental change away from what most salespeople are comfortable with.

The trick is to get to the benefit before you get to the feature. And the way you find the benefit is to keep asking yourself one question:

"How does that help my prospect?"

Keep going until you get to something that sounds almost too basic. Here's what that looks like:

The feature is: real-time dashboard with automated alerts.

"How does that help my prospect?" They see problems before customers call to complain.

"How does that help my prospect?" They fix issues the same day instead of three days later.

"How does that help my prospect?" They stop losing customers and their team stops firefighting.

Now present it from the bottom up: "Your team stops firefighting because you're catching delays the same day instead of finding out three days later. The way we do that is with a real-time dashboard that flags stuck orders automatically."

Benefits first. Features second. The benefit is what they care about. The feature is how you deliver it. Lead with the benefit and the feature will be close behind. But lead with the feature, and watch how easily the benefit gets lost. Before any presentation, ask yourself "How does that help my prospect?" for every feature you plan to discuss. By thinking about benefits before the call, you'll lead with them during the call.

Story → Scene → Translation: The Method for Each Bullet

Now that you know *what* to present (bullets, one at a time, hot bullet first) and *how* to frame it (benefits before features), you need a method for making each bullet presentation land—especially if you're showing a product, demo, or slide deck.

The method is: **Story → Scene → Translation.**

Story (30–60 seconds). Start each bullet's presentation with a micro-story: "We worked with a team that was seeing the same 90-day ramp problem you just described..." "A VP in your space told me she was spending half her week just trying to figure out which reps needed help..." Keep it short. Real situation. Real stakes. You're not doing a full case study. You're setting the scene in a way that feels familiar to them.

Scene (2–4 minutes). Then show one tight scene in your product or solution. One part of the workflow. One dashboard. One screen. You are not doing a tour. You are doing a scene. Talk to the person, not to the feature: "This is where your managers would go on Monday morning." "This is what you would see when you log in." Two to four minutes is enough to make the point. If you go longer, you're teaching a training class, not conveying value.

Translation (15–30 seconds). Never assume they'll connect the dots. End every scene by saying out loud what it means in their world: "For your frontline managers, this means they spend minutes, not hours, figuring out who to coach." "For you in finance, this is the moment you stop guessing ramp time and can actually forecast it." One or two sentences. Then stop.

Then you're into the check-in: "Where do you see that making the biggest difference?" Get your little yes. Check off the bullet. Move to the next one.

Story → Scene → Translation is the method. Bullets are the structure. Benefits before features is the rule. And little yeses are how you know it's working.

Bad vs. Good: A Live Demo Flow

To make this concrete, here's what a five-minute stretch of Convey can look like when it's done badly—and how it looks when it's driven by bullets, Story → Scene → Translation, and check-ins.

Bad: Generic feature tour.

Rep: "Okay, let me show you what we can do. This is the main dashboard. Up here you have your navigation bar. Over here are your filters. This tab shows you activity. This tab shows you reports. You can also export all of this to CSV. Down here you've got some charts, and if I click here you can drill down by region. Over on this side you can see user settings, and if I go into settings you'll see all the configuration options..."

Prospects nod politely, glance at other screens, and say "Looks powerful" at the end—because nothing was tied to their bullets.

Good: Bullet-driven scene.

Hot bullet: "Manual reporting eating 10 hours/week."

Rep: "You mentioned your managers are losing about ten hours a week just trying to pull reports together. What does that look like in a real week?" (Consequence Question)

Prospect: "Honestly, they're in spreadsheets half of Monday and most of Friday."

Rep: "So half their week is going to Excel instead of coaching. That's a big tax on the team." (Playback)

Rep: "We worked with a team that was in the same spot—Mondays and Fridays buried in spreadsheets instead of working with reps." (Story)

Rep: "Instead of opening six spreadsheets, your managers would open this." (Scene) Shows a single reporting view tied to their world for two to three minutes.

Rep: "For your managers, this means one click replaces ten hours of patchwork." (Translation)

Rep: "If your managers had this view last week, how would their Monday have looked different?" (Check-in)

Prospect: "Yeah. That would be huge."

Rep draws a line through "manual reporting eating 10 hrs/week" on the notepad and moves to the next bullet.

Same product. Same screen. The second version feels like their movie, not your feature tour. The amateur showed more. The professional showed what mattered.

You Are the Show, Not the Slides

Most reps—virtual or live—treat presentations like this: Slides full screen or projected huge. Product full screen on the wall. The rep: tiny box in the corner or literally off to the side.

In a real conference room, great presenters stand where people can see their face. They face the buyers more than the screen. They use the screen as backup, not the main event. Do the same online. Use a layout where you stay large on screen while presenting—overlay or presenter view—so you're not a postage stamp in the corner.

Whether in room or on video: You are the main visual. Behind or beside you are simple bullets and visuals that underline what you're saying. You are not narrating slides. You are telling a story, with a screen that happens to help.

People pay more attention to faces, eyes, and energy than to bullet points. Slides don't build trust. People do.

You Are the Energy in the Room

Before worrying about slides, stories, or check-ins, start with something more important: your energy.

People will say yes to you based more on your attitude and belief than on that graph on your slide. You can have the best product in the world. You can have a perfectly designed deck. You can execute every framework in this book flawlessly. But if you sound bored, unconvinced, or like you're just going through the motions, they will feel it. And they will say no. Not because your solution doesn't work. Because you didn't act like it matters.

The Fear That Kills Energy. Most reps know belief shows up in voice, face, and posture. But they're terrified of showing it. They think: "If I sound too excited, I'll seem salesy." "If I show I care too much, I'll look desperate." "Professionals are calm, neutral, controlled." So they flatten their voice. They remove the energy. They hide behind slides and data. And prospects check email.

Because nobody decides to move forward with someone who sounds unsure about their own solution.

Belief Is Not Desperation. Desperation sounds like: "Please just give this a chance." "I really need you to buy this." Belief sounds like: "This is going to change how your managers spend their Mondays—I've seen it happen." "When teams use this, onboarding drops from 90 days to 60. Every time." "The first time a client told me this saved them 10 hours a week, I didn't believe it. Then I saw the reports." One is needy. The other is confident certainty. Certainty is what people buy.

Before your next presentation, ask yourself: "What's the best outcome I've seen from this solution?" Not the marketing claim. Not the polished case study. The real story of a customer who told you, "This actually worked." Then tell that story like you mean it. Point at the screen with energy. Lean in when you show the part that matters. Let your voice go up when you talk about the result.

If you don't believe it, why should they?

Proof in Service of Bullets

Proof still matters. It just has to serve the bullets, not distract from them.

Throughout my career, the products I was most successful selling were the ones that had the most testimonials backing them up. I once had over thirty-five letters from happy customers—from doctors who loved the performance, nurses who found the product easy to maintain, office managers who saw great value, and patients who appreciated the technology. These letters were organized and ready to pull at a second's notice.

When a nurse raised a concern about maintenance, I pulled out three letters from other nurses who once felt the same way but were now satisfied. When a doctor questioned durability, I pulled out letters from physicians. These letters were gold. They gave me credibility I could find nowhere else.

For each major bullet, have one short testimonial or one simple number that supports what you just said. Use them after the prospect is already nodding on that bullet—not as your opening argument, but as confirmation.

Don't overdo the statistics. Use numbers only to strengthen the argument you're already winning. And know your audience—some prospects love charts and data. Others just need to hear that someone like them had the same concern and it worked out. Match the proof to the person.

Love All Bullets Equally

During Engage, you captured two types of bullets: Alter bullets—things they want to change—and Effective bullets—things that are already working well.

Most reps only focus on the Alter bullets. That's where the pain is, so that's where they spend all their time. But the Effective bullets matter just as much.

When a prospect tells you something is working, they're telling you what they're afraid of losing. Your transition line—"I think we can even improve on some of the things that are already working well for you"—addresses that fear directly. It tells them: you don't have to sacrifice what's good to fix what's broken.

Give every bullet its own presentation. The Alter bullets get Consequence Questions and benefits. The Effective bullets get confirmation and a brief explanation of how your solution protects or enhances what's already working. Both types earn little yeses. Both types build trust.

Floating Bullets

Sometimes Engage doesn't give you much. The prospect is tight-lipped, guarded, or just not a talker. You end up with one or two bullets when you needed four. A Floating Bullet is a topic you introduce during Convey that you believe is relevant—even though they didn't explicitly raise it. You float it by connecting it to something they did say:

"You mentioned that onboarding is taking too long. One thing we've seen in companies with that problem is that reporting also tends to be manual and time-consuming. Is that something you're dealing with too?"

If they bite, you just created a new bullet. Treat it exactly like the others: Consequence Question, benefit, feature, little yes, check it off. If they don't bite, let it go. You're floating, not forcing. Floating Bullets work because certain problems tend to travel together—and sometimes your prospect just needs you to name the one they hadn't thought to mention.

Convey by Role

You're still dealing with the same four people from Chapter 16. Each role needs at least one bullet presented in their language.

Operator: Story: "A training lead told me they were losing a full day a week just onboarding new reps." Scene: show the streamlined onboarding workspace. Translation: "For you, this means less chasing, more actual coaching." Check-in: "If you had this view tomorrow, what's the first thing you'd use it for?"

Owner: Story: "A VP of Sales realized ramp delays were killing her quarterly targets." Scene: show the metrics view that ties ramp time to revenue. Translation: "For you, this is about knowing if your ramp plan is working and what it does to your forecast." Check-in: "If you had this view last quarter, what would you have done differently?"

Gatekeeper: Story: "An IT leader at a healthcare company was terrified they couldn't prove who had completed which training." Scene: show the audit-ready report and permissions controls. Translation: "For IT, this means every training event is logged and exportable if you ever get audited." Check-in: "From an IT or compliance standpoint, would this remove some of the risk you're worried about?"

Absorber: Story: "A project manager told me, 'These things always land on my desk, and I'm the one everyone blames if rollout goes sideways.'" Scene: show the rollout checklist, timelines, and owner assignments. Translation: "For you, this means clearer ownership and fewer surprise tasks dumped on your plate." Check-in: "If this landed on your desk, would it make rollout feel more manageable or just like another burden?"

In enterprise deals, you'll often deliver variations of your Convey three to four times to different stakeholder groups. Same Story. Same Scene. Different Translation each time. You're not changing your message—you're shifting the emphasis based on who's in the room.

You don't need to run four separate demos. You do need to make sure each role gets at least one bullet aimed at their world.

Make This Style of Convey Automatic

As with everything else in PRECISE, you don't want Convey to depend on "remembering" in the moment. You want your mouth to feel weird if you're: Machine-gunning features without stories. Clicking through scenes without translations. Talking for ten minutes without a check-in. Presenting without checking off bullets.

Here's how to build the reflex.

Your Assignment: Day 19 — Show Less, Mean More

Drill 1: Feature Tour to Bullet-Driven Convey. Take a real presentation you've given recently. Write down the last 10 features you showed and the bullets the prospect actually cared about. Now rebuild: for each bullet, write a 30–60 second story, identify one scene, write a 1–2 sentence translation, and write one Consequence Question and one check-in question. Run a roleplay: Round 1, give the old feature tour. Round 2, give the same presentation using bullets. Feel which one lands.

Drill 2: HDTHMP Drill. Pick three features of your product. For each one, ask yourself "How does that help my prospect?" four or five times until you arrive at the core benefit. Then practice presenting each one from the bottom up: benefit first, feature last. Do this until leading with benefits feels more natural than leading with features.

Drill 3: Check-In Cadence. Pick one bullet and one scene. Practice this mini-sequence five times: Re-state the bullet, ask a Consequence Question, tell a 30–60 second story, show the scene for 2–3 minutes, translate in 1–2 sentences, ask a check-in question. Each time, vary your check-in. You're training your brain that bullets and check-ins go together—and that no bullet is done until you get a little yes.

Drill 4: Presence and Talk-Time Audit. Record one real presentation. After the call, review: How much did you talk vs. how much they talked? How many genuine check-ins did you ask (not "Any questions?")? Did you sound like you actually believed what you were showing? On your next three presentations, aim to reduce your talk time and add at least one directed check-in per bullet.

Show What Matters, Believe What You Show

Here's the through line: In Chapter 13, you learned to convey what you do in 30 seconds without killing curiosity. In this chapter, you learned to stretch that same idea across a full meeting—without drowning anyone in features.

You are not a tour guide for your product. You are a precision-guided weapon—armed with bullets your prospect gave you, loaded hot bullet first, and delivering each one with benefits, stories, and little yeses until the whole thing builds to a conclusion that feels inevitable.

Because here's the truth most reps never learn:

Prospects don't buy features. They buy belief that those features will make their lives better.

And they buy that belief from reps who actually sound like they believe it.

Amateurs click through every feature and hope something sticks. Pros pick their bullets, tell real stories, translate clearly, and check in often enough to hear the truth.

Each bullet gets its own presentation. A bunch of little yeses become one big yes.

Day 19 begins now.

CHAPTER 20

Indecision

Knock Their Ass Off the Fence—But Knock Yours Off First

Let's clear something up right away.

When a prospect hesitates—pushes back—says "I need to think about it" or gives you some version of "not yet"—they are not rejecting you. They're doing what normal, intelligent humans do when they feel uncertainty.

Indecision is not the end of the sale. It's a moment inside the sale. And how you handle that moment determines whether the conversation moves forward—or quietly dies while you tell yourself, "That was a good meeting."

Two People Need to Get Off the Fence

There are two parties that need to be decision-makers in any sales call. One is the prospect. The other is you.

Most salespeople look at selling as an exchange of information. While information sharing is necessary, your objective is not to deliver information. **Your objective is to get a decision about your prospect's intentions in getting involved with your solution.**

Prospects by nature often fear decision-making. Their walls of defense are fortified with bricks of indecision. It is your job to break down those walls and knock their ass off the fence. But you must knock your ass off first.

In my seminars, nine out of ten students tell me they wish they felt more comfortable when it came time to ask for the order. Not one has ever told me their biggest challenge is that they "close too much." Most believe they have a tendency to just let a sale hang out there and float in the wind, hoping the pieces fall into place.

They won't. The most efficient sales call is one where a decision about getting involved with your solution is made. That decision is hopefully a "yes." But a "no" is fine too, as long as some decision is made.

You must make the decision to ask for a decision.

The Posture That Ignites Decisions

Sir William Osler, the physician who helped found Johns Hopkins Hospital, spoke about a quality called *imperturbability*—coolness and presence of mind under all circumstances, calmness amid storm, clearness of judgment in moments of grave peril. He said the physician who lacks it—who betrays indecision and worry, who shows that he is flustered in ordinary emergencies—loses rapidly the confidence of his patients.

Replace "physician" with "salesperson." Replace "patients" with "prospects." The truth doesn't change.

Be decisive and prospects will follow. Even when your customer is perturbed, you must be the calm in the storm. This calmness provides comfort and confidence and produces a climate for action and decision. George Patton had imperturbability. You need it too.

The way you conduct yourself when a prospect has a doubt or concern has a direct impact on the outcome of the call. Your believability and credibility are tested every time a customer says, "But the competition says..." or "I'm not sure the ROI is there." Get frazzled or defensive and your prospect will have a hard time overlooking it. Stay cool, get a gleam in your eye, and address those doubts—and the importance of those doubts is often lessened before you even open your mouth.

Indecision Wastes Time—Yours and Theirs

Salespeople waste countless hours making "follow-up" calls on previously visited prospects. While follow-ups are sometimes necessary, they often do nothing to advance the sale. They fill up your calendar but don't fill your bank account. Indecision is responsib_e for most of those wasted calls.

Making a decision to ask for a decision—during the first sales call, or the first few depending on your cycle—can save immeasurable hours. Hours that could be spent prospecting for new business.

And sometimes customers can't decide how to let you down easy, so they string you along, spewing misinformation while they're killing you softly. Well, soft killings take too much time. A "no" today is worth more than six months of "maybe." Every week you spend chasing a deal that was never going to close is a week you didn't spend finding one that would.

The Indianapolis 500 Sales Wreck

I once had a doctor prospect whose office sat directly across the street from the Indianapolis Motor Speedway. He was an ear, nose, and throat physician interested in our flexible, fiber-optic rhinolaryngoscope—the skinny scope that looks like a black noodle that gets inserted into the nose and down the throat to diagnose head and neck problems.

I did a demonstration and impressed him with my nasal knowledge. He drove that scope through the narrow turns of my nostrils like Mario Andretti cruising the speedway after throwing back a twelve-pack of Pabst Blue Ribbon. He wasn't very good at the procedure, but at least he wore a smile as he tortured me.

After shooting the breeze for about an hour, touching on everything from tonsils to carburetors, I thought the sale was in the bag. He told me he liked the scope and to leave some information. He promised to get back to me by the end of the week. I believed him.

At no time during that call did I ask him to make a decision about buying the scope.

One week later I made a three-hour drive south from Chicago to follow up. Receptionist said he was too busy. Six unreturned phone calls and three more live "He's busy" responses later, I was catching on. He had a deal with another manufacturer. Between me not asking for a decision and his inability to tell me directly, I wasted three hours down, three hours back, six voicemails, eight follow-ups, and one ticked-off receptionist. All because I didn't have the guts to ask a simple question while I was sitting right in front of him.

The Five Land Mines That Cause Indecision

Those bricks of indecision are not random. There are five specific reasons prospects resist moving forward. Identify which one is blocking you and you can address it directly instead of guessing.

1. Lack of Information. When a customer has a question that can't be answered, that's often enough to prevent them from moving forward. This is why Preparation matters. Never let "I'm not sure" or "I'll get back to you on that" be responsible for a blown sale.

2. Lack of Emotion. People buy emotionally and defend it logically. If your Convey was flat, monotone, and lifeless, don't be surprised when the prospect's response matches. Energy forces prospects to either enthusiastically say yes or enthusiastically say no. Either way, it's a decision.

3. Lack of Credibility. Prospects need to believe that what you're saying is true. If you haven't earned their respect and trust, it's difficult to get them to commit. If the prospect doesn't trust the messenger, the message doesn't matter.

4. Lack of Urgency. Without urgency, prospects rarely buy. Your job during Engage was to use questions to transform hidden needs into observable ones. If you did that well, urgency is already present. If you skipped it, this land mine is waiting for you.

5. Doubts and Concerns. They feel like speed bumps, but if you handle them correctly, you can use them to create urgency. When prospects share a concern, they're posing a challenge. A challenge is an open door to prove yourself. If your prospect has a concern, you always want to know about it.

The Benefits vs. Concerns Scale

Pretend you're bringing a scale into every sales call. On one side are all the benefits your solution provides. On the other side are all the doubts and concerns. At the end of your call, the benefit side must clearly outweigh the concern side. It doesn't need to be empty—it just needs to weigh less.

If you've done the first four PRECISE Actions well, you've already loaded the benefit side. Each bullet got its own presentation and its own little yes. Each little yes is a weight on the benefit side. Once the scale is tipping in one direction, it's hard to reverse. A few weights on the concern side won't matter—because your PRECISE benefits weigh a hell of a lot more.

And when your competition really is better in a specific area? Give that weight to your prospect. Let them put it on the concern side. Then make sure the benefit side still wins. Trying to deny a legitimate competitive advantage makes you look dishonest. Acknowledging it and outweighing it makes you look confident.

SHARP in the Warm Meeting

In Chapter 14, you learned SHARP for handling indecision during prospecting calls—surface-level brush-offs designed to get you off the phone. In a warm meeting, indecision looks different. It's deeper, more nuanced, and it shows up mid-presentation.

"Your competitor does this part better." "I'm not sure the ROI justifies the switch." "We tried something like this before and it didn't work." "I like what I'm seeing, but I need to think about it."

These aren't brush-offs. These are real humans processing real uncertainty. The framework doesn't change—Stop, Hear, Ask, Respond, Pack—but the depth does. And your composure can't waver.

The biggest mistake reps make in this moment is skipping the A. They hear the concern, they think they know what it means, and they jump straight to their response. That's how you address the wrong concern—and create a new one in the process.

The Concern I Thought I Heard

I used to sell a video colposcope—a magnified video camera on a mobile stand used for cervical examinations. Traditionally done with an optical scope that resembles a microscope, our video system projected the image onto a monitor. Physicians were skeptical. Clarity is everything during this exam.

I was presenting to a large OB/GYN practice in Chicago. Things were going great through Prepare, Respect and Trust, Engage, and Convey. Then one physician said: "I'm concerned that I won't get a three-dimensional image when looking at the cervix on a video monitor, as I do with my optical scope."

Thinking I knew exactly what he meant, I skipped Stop, Hear, and Ask and went straight to my response: "Doctor, many OB/GYNs using our system have found the clarity on the video monitor is sufficient to notice any subtle tissue changes."

He paused. "Oh. I was actually more concerned about getting a three-dimensional image for when I take biopsies. I'm afraid I'll misjudge how much tissue to take. But now that you mention visualization, I guess that's a concern as well."

I blew it. By skipping the A, I addressed the wrong concern and handed him a brand new one. He walked in with one worry. He left with two.

Here's how I should have handled it. After he raised the concern: Stop. Shut up. Hear everything he's trying to say. Then, because the concern isn't specific enough, ask: "Doctor, can you help me better understand how not having a three-dimensional image will affect your procedure?" He tells me it's about biopsies. Now I know exactly what to address. And I don't create a second concern in the process.

Even when you think you know what the customer means, ask for clarification.

Velvet Conviction

Doubts and concerns arise quickly and out of nowhere. You need to overcome them with what I call *velvet conviction*—a strong, decisive response delivered in a yielding way. You attack the doubts quickly without attacking your prospect.

Example: you're mid-presentation and a customer says, "Your competition was in here yesterday and says your quality is horrible." Every cell in your body wants to curl up your top lip and call the lying idiot a...well...lying idiot. Don't. Take a breath. Count to three. Use your questioning skills to get to the bottom of it. The goal is honesty—because in that honesty is the key to the sale. If you act defensively, they'll be too uncomfortable to be honest with you.

Velvet conviction is confidence without arrogance. It's the calm that makes your prospect think, "This person has heard this before and isn't rattled." That reaction builds more credibility than any slide in your deck.

Challenge Them to Choose Action Over Comfort

The colposcope story shows you what happens when SHARP goes wrong. Here's what it looks like when it goes right—and more importantly, when you use it to challenge the prospect to move forward without making them feel pushed.

You're three bullets into a warm meeting. The prospect has been nodding. You've collected two little yeses. Then:

"I like what I'm seeing, but I need to run this by my team before we do anything."

Most reps hear that and immediately retreat: "Of course! Take your time. I'll send over everything you need." They walk out feeling polite. Two weeks later they're writing "just circling back" emails into the void. That rep didn't lose to a competitor. They lost to the status quo. And they helped the prospect stay there.

Here's how a PRECISE rep handles the same moment.

Stop. Pause. Let the words land without reacting.

Hear. "Totally understand. Most teams we work with go through the same process."

Ask. And this is where the challenge lives—not in a statement, but in a question. "Help me understand—when you say run it by the team, is that more about getting buy-in on the solution itself, or is it about getting approval on the budget?"

That question does something most reps never do: it separates the real concern from the polite stall. The prospect now has to tell you which wall you're actually hitting. Nine times out of ten, they'll tell you.

"Honestly, it's more the budget. I like the solution. I just don't know if we can swing it this quarter."

Now you know. And now you can challenge—with velvet conviction.

Respond. "That's actually the most common conversation we have at this stage. Let me ask you something. You told me earlier that the current process is costing you roughly ten hours a week in manual reporting. If we don't solve that this quarter, what does that cost you over the next six months?"

That's a **cost-of-inaction question.** You're not arguing about budget. You're making them calculate the cost of doing nothing. You're using their own numbers—the ones they gave you during Engage—to challenge the assumption that waiting is free. It never is. And when they do the math out loud, they feel it.

The prospect pauses. "Yeah...that's probably forty weeks of wasted hours. That's a lot."

"It is. And here's what most teams in your position do. Instead of the full rollout, they start with one department—prove the ROI internally—then expand. The initial investment is smaller and you've got results to point to when the bigger budget conversation happens."

That's a **reduced-risk path.** You didn't discount. You didn't beg. You offered a way forward that respects their constraint while keeping the deal alive.

Pack. "Does that feel like a realistic path for your team?"

"Yeah, that could actually work. Let me talk to finance about the phased option."

That prospect walked in ready to stall. They walked out with a next step. Not because you pressured them—but because you asked the questions that made staying the same feel more expensive than moving forward.

That's the discipline. Challenge them with their own words. Make inaction expensive with their own numbers. Then offer a path that removes the excuse. You're not closing. You're leading.

Script Your Five

Here's the uncomfortable reality. Most salespeople hear the same five objections over and over again. Not fifty. Not a hundred. Five. And instead of preparing for those five moments, they wing it every time.

Write down the five concerns you hear most. Write them exactly as your prospects say them. Then develop a response to each one—draw it up as if you were Steven Spielberg writing an Academy Award-winning script. Then rehearse it like your favorite actor preparing for a shoot.

I've done this for years and it has meant tens of thousands of dollars to me. I almost look forward to hearing a concern I'm prepared for, because it gives me a chance to deliver the lines I practiced.

"I hate canned responses...they sound so canned." They only sound canned when they're not practiced well enough and often enough.

There are differences between soap opera actors and Academy Award winners, and those differences are ability and practice. I know you have the ability. Now it takes practice.

AI Assist: Before you practice live, use AI as a sparring partner. Feed it your prospect's industry, the concern, and your draft response. Ask it to punch holes in your answer—then rewrite. It won't replace the live roleplay, but it'll make sure you're not walking into practice with a weak script.

The Detail Question

Once you've resolved a concern and packed it with agreement, move the conversation forward with a Detail Question—a question that takes the prospect mentally from "considering your solution" to "using your solution." After resolving the doctor's concern about biopsies: "Doctor, I'm glad you're confident the system will work. Now I'm curious—in which exam room will you be performing these?" If they start telling you specifics—which room, which team members, which workflow—the benefit side of the scale is winning.

Your Assignment: Prepare for the Moments That Matter

Drill 1: Write Your Five. List the five concerns you hear most in warm meetings. Write them exactly as your prospects say them. Then write one full SHARP response for each: the pause, the acknowledgment, one clarifying question, a twenty-to-thirty-second response, and an alignment question. Practice each one out loud five times. Record yourself. Did I actually pause? Did I ask just one question? Did my response stay under thirty seconds?

Drill 2: The Scale Audit. Think about your last three deals that stalled. For each one, draw the Benefits vs. Concerns scale. How many little yeses did you collect before the concern showed up? If the benefit side wasn't heavy enough, the problem wasn't the objection—it was that your Convey didn't load enough weight first.

Drill 3: Velvet Conviction Roleplay. Grab a partner. Have them throw your five concerns at you randomly, mid-presentation.

Practice staying calm, pausing, and responding with velvet conviction. Score yourself: Did I flinch? Did I get defensive? Did I sound like I'd heard this before and wasn't rattled?

Indecision Is a Signal, Not a Stop Sign

Indecision is not a threat. It's a signal that the prospect is still thinking. Still engaged. Still in the conversation.

When you're prepared for that moment—when nothing they say surprises you—you stop fearing objections and start expecting them.

Amateurs panic when concerns show up. Pros expect them—and stay calm when they do.

That's when selling gets simpler. That's when prospects start trusting you, not because you had all the answers, but because you handled uncertainty better than anyone else they talk to.

Day 20 begins now.

CHAPTER 21

Secure Agreement and Explore

Close with Structure, Not Hope

Let me tell you about the time I ran a perfect meeting and still lost the deal—because I was too scared to talk about money.

The discovery was clean. The demo landed. They nodded at everything. They said, "This could really help us."

Then the VP asked: "So what does this cost?"

And I froze. I hadn't prepared the numbers. I hadn't thought through options. I was terrified of hearing no.

So I said: "Let me pull together a proposal and send it over." She said: "Sure, that works." I walked out feeling like I'd dodged a bullet.

Two weeks later, after three "just circling back" emails, I realized: I hadn't dodged anything. I'd just postponed the rejection.

If you don't secure agreement when momentum is high, you're not being polite. You're being a coward. And cowards don't close deals.

Back on Day 15, you learned how to Secure Agreement to get meetings on the calendar. You didn't say "let me know what works." You said: "Thursday at 10 or Friday at 2. Which works better?" You offered structured choice instead of vague deferral—and it worked.

Now you're going to use the same tool—structured choice—to close. Not to get the meeting. To get the commitment.

Why Reps Avoid Closing

Most reps don't avoid commitment because they're lazy. They avoid it because it feels like standing on a trap door. One wrong word and the whole thing blows up. So they stay vague, send proposals, and hope the buyer decides on their own. They won't.

They're unprepared. Great discovery, great demo—no plan for what comes next. When the buyer asks, "What does this cost?" they panic and say, "I'll send you a proposal." Translation: "I didn't respect this moment enough to prepare for it."

They're afraid the relationship will change. For thirty minutes, you've been on the same side of the table. The moment you ask for commitment—money, a pilot, a VP meeting—reps think: "Now I'm a salesperson." So they postpone it and let the relationship die slowly instead.

They confuse patience with avoidance. "I don't want to be pushy. Let them think about it." Meanwhile, the buyer moves on to the next fire and your "hot lead" disappears under forty-seven other priorities. Patience isn't the problem. Vagueness is.

They've been ghosted before. They've sent proposals that vanished. They've written "just circling back" until they want to puke. So when a buyer says, "Send me a proposal," they cling to that as progress. But hope without structure is just another word for ghost mode.

Every one of these fears feels protective. Every one of them is killing your pipeline.

The Rep Who Stopped Sending Proposals Into the Void

One of our AEs, Michelle, had a brutal pattern: killer discovery, solid demo, then "Let me send you a proposal." Her proposal-to-close rate: eight percent.

When we reviewed her calls, she did everything right until the final five minutes. Then she'd say: "So what do you think? Should I put together some numbers?" Buyers would say: "Yeah, send something over." Michelle would spend three hours building a beautiful proposal. Send it. Follow up. Follow up again. Ghost mode.

We gave her one new framework: the Three Choice Close.

Confirm value first. Present three structured options. Ask: "Based on these three, which makes the most sense for you?"

First call using it: the buyer said, "Probably the 24-month option. Let me confirm with our CFO by Friday." Michelle followed up Friday. CFO approved. Deal closed the following week.

Within two months, her close rate went from eight percent to twenty-nine. Same product. Same buyers. Different final five minutes.

The Psychology Behind Three Choices

Buyers don't all need the same thing to say yes. Some want to do what everyone else does. Some want the best. Some just need a way to say yes without blowing up their budget. Your job is to give all three a place to land.

That's why you don't present Good, Better, Best. You present **Better → Best → Good** and frame them like this:

Better: "Most people like you." "Most clinics your size go with Option 1." Social proof. Normal. Responsible. Anchors the conversation in the middle, not at the cheapest option.

Best: "Those who want the most." "Others who want the most comprehensive package go with Option 2." Speaks to status and control. Feels like an intentional upgrade, not a crazy leap.

Good: "Limited or fixed budget." "Smaller clinics on a fixed budget go with Option 3." Gives budget-constrained buyers a face-saving way to say yes. Quietly pulls comparison back toward the middle.

After you lay out the three options, you don't ask, "What do you think?" You say: "Based on these three, which one makes the most sense for you?" You're holding up three mirrors and letting them decide which one they see themselves in—just like "Thursday at 10 or Friday at 2."

The Three Choice Financial Presentation

When the decision involves money, you don't want one number. You want three clear choices. Not tricks. Not pressure. Just structure.

Step 1: Confirm the value first. Never show price into a vacuum. After your Convey, ask: "We've talked about how this could improve patient outcomes and make your workflow more efficient. Do you still feel that way?" If they say no, you have a value problem, not a pricing problem. Go back. If they say yes: "Great. Then the only question left is whether it makes financial sense. Let's look at a few ways to do that."

Step 2: Present three options. Frame them the same way every time. "Most clinics your size go with a 24-month program at about $400 per month. Others decide to make the total investment outright at $9,900. Smaller clinics on a fixed budget go with a 48-month program at about $220 per month. Based on these three, which would make the most sense for your practice?"

Step 3: Ask a clean, simple question. Your close line is boring on purpose: "Based on these three, which one makes the most sense for you?" Not: "What do you think?" or "Any questions?" Those invite commentary. You want a choice.

Two Worked Examples You Can Steal

Here are two complete Three Choice presentations—one financing-based, one product-based. Study the structure. Adapt the labels to your world. The framework doesn't change.

Example 1: Financing Options (Medical Device)

"Let's see if this makes financial sense. There are three ways clinics your size typically handle this."

Option 1 (Better): "Most clinics your size go with a 24-month program at about $400 per month. That gives you full access to the system, training for your staff, and ongoing support. It's the most popular choice because it balances investment with cash flow."

Option 2 (Best): "Others decide to make the total investment outright at $9,900. You own the system day one, there's no monthly payment, and you lock in today's pricing. Clinics that have the budget available usually prefer this because it's the lowest total cost."

Option 3 (Good): "Smaller clinics on a tighter budget go with a 48-month program at about $220 per month. The monthly number is lower, which makes it easier to absorb. It takes longer to pay off, but it gets you started without straining cash flow."

"Based on these three, which one makes the most sense for your practice?"

Example 2: Product Tiers (Software Platform)

"Let's look at the three packages teams your size typically choose."

Option 1 (Better): "Most teams your size go with the Professional tier at $850 per month. That includes the core platform, reporting dashboards, and dedicated onboarding. It covers everything you described needing during our conversation."

Option 2 (Best): "Teams that want the most comprehensive solution go with the Enterprise tier at $1,400 per month. That adds advanced analytics, custom integrations with your existing systems, and a dedicated success manager. It's built for organizations scaling across multiple departments."

Option 3 (Good): "Teams on a fixed budget or running a pilot go with the Starter tier at $500 per month. It's the core platform with standard support. Most teams that start here upgrade within six months once they see the results."

"Based on how you described your needs, which of these three makes the most sense?"

Two different industries. Two different structures. Same framework: Better first, Best second, Good third. One clean question. Adapt the labels and numbers to your world, but don't change the order and don't add a fourth option. Three is the number. Three gives them a place to land without overwhelming them.

Trade, Don't Concede

The Three Choice Close gets you to a number. But what happens when they say, "That's more than we budgeted" or "Can you do any better?" That's negotiation. And most reps panic, drop price immediately, and leave money on the table. Pros negotiate by trading value, not bleeding margin.

The core principle: never move on price or terms without getting something back.

Before you sit down, prepare three things. First, what they'll ask for—lower monthly number, faster implementation, premium features at mid-tier price. Second, what you can give— implementation priority, extra training sessions, better support tier for the first ninety days, flexible payment terms. Third, what you'll ask for in return—longer contract term, more locations in scope, earlier start date, being a public reference, warm introductions to peer organizations.

The Give/Get Framework. When they ask for something, don't say yes. Don't say no. Say: "If we could do X, would you be willing to Y?" You're not capitulating. You're trading.

Buyer: "Your price is higher than expected. Can you come down?" You: "I hear you. Budget is always real. If we adjusted the term to 48 months, that brings the monthly investment down significantly. If we could make that work, would you be comfortable committing to the longer term?" You didn't discount. You traded term for monthly affordability.

Buyer: "Can you throw in the premium training?" You: "We could add premium training. Most clients who do that also commit to an extended support agreement because they use the advanced features more deeply. If we included the premium training, would you be open to a 24-month support term?" They get an upgrade. You get commitment.

233

When to hold the line. Not every ask deserves a trade. Sometimes the right answer is a calm, respectful no. "I get why you're asking. If we moved to that level of discount, we'd be absorbing the cost, and that changes how we can support you. That wouldn't be fair to either of us." You're not defensive. You're explaining why the trade doesn't make sense—and pointing back to a structured option.

Four truths about price. First, you will lose some deals on price. It's reality, not failure. Second, customers are trained to ask for a lower price. Asking doesn't mean they won't pay full price. Third, your attitude about price affects the price. Say the number like you believe it's fair. Hesitation invites negotiation. Fourth, never move on price without being asked. Salespeople often lower price preemptively. That's self-inflicted damage.

Securing Agreement to Non-Financial Next Steps

Not every next step is about money. Sometimes it's a pilot, a technical proof of concept, an executive presentation, or a budget discussion. The principle is the same: structured choice beats "let me know."

Pilot: "Based on what we've discussed, the typical next step is a pilot. Most teams your size do one of two things: two sites for sixty days, or one site for thirty days to see quick results. Which makes more sense for you?"

Executive Briefing: "Since this impacts regional targets, the next step is usually a short briefing with your VP. Teams handle it two ways: you and I present together for twenty minutes, or you present internally first and I join for Q&A. Which would work better?"

Same pattern every time: name the natural next step, offer two structured ways to do it, secure agreement to one.

Own the Close

Everything from the Convey chapter still applies: you are the show, not the spreadsheet. Your energy sells the decision as much as the logic.

Say the number with conviction. Say it like your own address: "The total investment is $9,900." Then stop.

Keep the visual simple. Three options, clear labels, one line each. No seventeen-row matrix.

Watch their face, not your notes. Say the number, then look at them—whether that's across the table or into the camera.

Handle the silence. After "Which one makes the most sense?" count to five in your head. Don't rescue them from deciding.

Create Urgency So the Deal Doesn't Drift

You've presented three options. They're leaning forward. They like what they see. And then: "This is great. Let me take this back to the team and we'll circle back next quarter."

That deal just died. It doesn't know it yet, but it's dead. Because "next quarter" is where good meetings go to disappear. Calendars fill. Priorities shift. The urgency you spent forty-five minutes building evaporates in seventy-two hours.

Your job isn't to pressure them into buying today. Your job is to make waiting feel expensive. And you do that with tools, not tricks.

Use their own timeline against drift. During Engage, you asked about deadlines, goals, and pain. Now use those answers. "You mentioned you need this operational before your Q3 rollout. If we start the process next week, we hit that window. If we wait until next quarter, we're looking at a Q4 start—which puts you a full cycle behind." You're not manufacturing urgency. You're reminding them of urgency they already told you about.

Attach a cost to delay. This is the cost-of-inaction question you used in Chapter 20, now applied to the close. "You said the current process costs your team roughly ten hours a week. Every month we wait is another forty hours your team doesn't get back. What does that cost you over a quarter?" Let them do the math. When they hear their own number, it stings more than anything you could say.

Anchor to an external event. Implementation timelines, fiscal year budgets, regulatory deadlines, seasonal demand—any external clock that exists independently of you. "Our implementation team is booking into March right now. If we lock this in by Friday, I can hold your slot. After that, we're looking at April." That's not pressure. That's logistics. And logistics are real.

Offer a reason to move now. Not a discount—a reason. "If we start this month, I can include the onboarding support package at no additional cost because my implementation team has bandwidth. That goes away once they're booked." You're not cheapening the deal. You're adding value to speed.

The common thread: every urgency tool uses information they already gave you or conditions that already exist. You're not inventing pressure. You're organizing the truth so the cost of waiting becomes impossible to ignore.

AI Assist: Before your next closing conversation, feed AI your three pricing options and your prospect's industry. Ask it to roleplay as a budget-conscious buyer who pushes back on price and tries to delay. Practice your Give/Get responses and urgency anchors until they feel natural, not rehearsed.

Explore: The Best Time to Get a Yes Is Right After a Yes

After they commit, something happens that most reps completely miss. The prospect's guard drops. The tension of deciding is gone. They feel good about the choice they just made. They're in a state of forward motion—and forward motion is the most valuable currency in sales.

The best time to get somebody to say yes is when they just said yes.

This is not manipulation. It's psychology. A person who just made a decision is in decision-making mode. Their brain is wired for action, not resistance. They're thinking about implementation, about results, about what's next. If you let that moment pass—if you shake hands, pack up, and walk out—you're leaving the highest-belief moment of the entire relationship on the table.

Explore the Start: Pilot vs. Full, Location A vs. B

The first thing to Explore after a commitment is how they want to begin. This isn't a separate close. It's a natural extension of the one they just made—and it's where Explore earns its place in the chapter title.

Most buyers don't need to be convinced to start. They need help choosing *how* to start. And the moment they pick an option from your three choices, that question is already alive in their head. If you don't shape it, they'll either overthink it internally or default to the slowest path.

Use structured choice again—same tool, smaller decision.

Pilot vs. full rollout: "Most teams your size handle the launch one of two ways. Some start with a full rollout across all locations so everyone's on the same system from day one. Others start with a pilot at one or two sites, prove the results, then expand. Which feels more realistic for your team?"

Location A vs. Location B: "You mentioned your main office and your south campus both feel this problem. If we started with one, which site would give us the fastest proof of results?"

Phased timeline: "Would you rather go live in thirty days with the core features, or take sixty days and launch with everything configured? Most teams prefer the faster start because early wins build internal momentum."

Every one of these questions does the same thing: it moves the conversation from "should we do this?" to "how do we do this?" That's the mental shift that separates a signed deal from a stalled one. And it's Explore in action—not expanding to new buyers, but expanding the commitment into a concrete plan.

Cross-Sell: Plant the Seed While Belief Is High

Cross-selling after a commitment isn't about squeezing more out of the deal. It's about solving the next problem while they're already in problem-solving mode.

The key is a hook—a single sentence that connects what they just bought to something adjacent they haven't thought about yet.

Same location, different problem: "Since you're rolling this out in your main clinic, I should mention—most practices that implement this also start looking at how they handle [adjacent workflow]. It's not urgent today, but it's worth a fifteen-minute conversation down the road. Would you be open to that?"

Same problem, different location: "You mentioned your satellite offices deal with the same issue. Once you see results here, would it make sense for me to put together a quick comparison for those sites? No commitment—just so you have it when the conversation comes up internally."

Next problem in the chain: "Now that the diagnostic side is handled, the next thing teams like yours usually run into is [downstream issue]. I'm not suggesting we tackle it now, but I'd love to show you a quick look at how other clients have approached it. Would that be useful?"

Notice the pattern. Every hook does three things: connects to what they just bought, names a specific adjacent problem, and asks for a small next step—not a commitment. You're not closing again. You're opening the next door while this one is still warm.

If they say not yet, you don't push. You planted a seed in the highest-belief soil available. It'll grow on its own. If they say yes, you just expanded the relationship in sixty seconds.

Referrals: Turn One Yes Into Two Conversations

Most reps never ask for referrals. The ones who do ask at the wrong time—when the prospect is stressed, undecided, or barely paying attention. Right after a commitment is the right time, because the prospect is doing something rare: they're actively endorsing your solution in their own mind.

The question is simple: "One more quick question—who else in your world is wrestling with the same issues you were dealing with before this?"

Don't say "Do you know anyone who might be interested?" That's vague and easy to deflect. Ask about a specific pain—the one they just solved. That triggers a face, a name, a conversation they had last week.

If they name someone: "Would you be open to a quick intro email? Just so I can see if it's worth a conversation. If it's not a fit, no harm done."

If they hesitate: "No pressure at all. If someone comes to mind later, just shoot me their name and I'll take it from there."

A referral from a buyer who just said yes carries more weight than a hundred cold calls. Their name opens the door. Their experience starts the trust. You're not prospecting from scratch—you're prospecting from proof.

In Chapter 16, you learned to Explore the buying committee—mapping stakeholders, getting to the real decision-maker. That was Explore *before* the decision. This is Explore *after* the decision. The first Explore widens the room. This one widens the relationship. Both are the final letter in PRECISE for a reason: the sale doesn't end when they say yes. That's where the next sale begins.

Your Assignment: Close with Structure, Not Hope

Drill 1: Three Choice Close. Script your value confirmation, three real pricing or next-step options, and your closing question: "Based on these three, which makes the most sense for you?" Record yourself delivering it. Fix one thing each take—voice drop on the number, nervous filler words, rushing through the options.

Drill 2: Negotiation Prep. Before your next five closing conversations, write down three things: what they'll ask for, what you can give, and what you'll ask for in return. Practice: "If we could do X, would you be willing to Y?" until it rolls off your tongue.

Drill 3: Indecision at the Close. Roleplay "I need to think about it" with a partner. Practice naming it, asking one clarifying question, and reshaping to a smaller structured next step. Don't argue. Don't retreat. Redirect.

Drill 4: The Sixty-Second Explore. After your next three closes—real or practice—don't pack up. Deliver one cross-sell hook and one referral ask. Time yourself. If it takes longer than sixty seconds, you're overcomplicating it. The goal is a seed, not a second presentation.

The Top

You've spent twenty days rebuilding how you sell. You know how to prepare before the call, earn respect in the first six seconds, engage with questions that uncover truth, convey your solution with bullets that land, handle indecision without flinching, secure agreement with structured choice, and explore the room and the relationship.

You're not the same rep you were on Day 1.

Most salespeople wing it and wonder why deals die. You built a system—and now you know why buyers say yes.

This was never a motivation book. It was a manual. A playbook. A framework you can run in real conversations with real buyers, in an environment that doesn't hand out second chances easily.

Some of what you learned confirmed what you already did well. Some of it contradicted habits you've carried for years. A few lessons probably stung a little.

Good.

The goal was never to make you feel good about where you were. The goal was to give you a repeatable way to get where you want to go.

Welcome to the top.

THE PAYOFF

The PRECISE Call Book

This is where PRECISE stops being a good idea in your head and becomes ink on paper.

Most salespeople walk out of calls with a feeling, not a fact. "Good." "Bad." "Felt okay." Feelings don't tell you why a call worked or fell apart. They don't show you which PRECISE Actions you actually executed and which ones you skipped entirely. And they don't help you get better on the next call.

The PRECISE Call Book fixes that. It gives you: A place to plan the call. A place to stay oriented during the call. A place to tell yourself the truth afterward. Not with essays. With structure.

This is not a script. It's a guardrail—so you don't drive the call off a cliff.

Why a Call Book?

The Call Book does two jobs—one during the call, one after.

During the call it works as a quiet cheat sheet. If you blank out, feel pressure, or sense yourself drifting, you just look down. The next PRECISE Action is sitting there waiting for you. No panic. No babbling. No guessing what comes next.

After the call it becomes a self-evaluation tool that exposes patterns you'd never see otherwise. In a few lines you can see: Prepared... yes. Asked enough questions... no. Secured agreement... maybe.

You don't need to write a novel. In fact, the shorter and more honest your notes are, the faster you improve. A clear objective at the top. A few bullets on what worked. A couple of "Forgot to..." reminders. Repeat that process call after call, and your career changes—not because you're smarter, but because you're more honest.

If a rep gets lost mid-call, they don't spiral. They look down. The process is right there.

Two Tabs. Four Sheets.

The PRECISE Call Book is divided into two sections: Cold Prospecting—for calls where they didn't see you coming. Warm Prospecting—for people who know your name or raised their hand.

During Call Sheets quietly prompt you through: Prepare, Respect & Trust, Engage, CLEAR questions, Convey, Indecision, Secure, Explore.

Post-Call Evaluation Sheets walk you back through the same PRECISE Actions so you can quickly mark what you did well—and what you flat-out missed.

If you're an SDR making high-volume dials, you don't fill one out for every voicemail. Use it for real conversations and booked meetings. If you're a field rep or account executive, aim to evaluate every meaningful live visit or Zoom call.

In your first 20 days, you'll probably write more "Forgot to..." notes than "Great job." That's not failure. That's awareness.

The Real Value: Self-Evaluation

The biggest benefit of the PRECISE Call Book isn't that it helps you sound smooth. It makes you honest.

After each call, the page quietly asks: Did you really prepare—or did you wing it? Did you earn Respect & Trust—or rush into your pitch? Did you stay curious—or start talking too soon? Did you handle indecision calmly—or get defensive? Did you secure a real next step—or just "check in"?

As you focus on improving one or two PRECISE Actions per call, the pages change. The negatives shrink. The positives grow. When managers ride with reps 20 days into the program and flip through their Call Books, they don't need dashboards or speeches. They can see the improvement—call by call—until there's barely anything left to write except: "Great job."

A Modern Call Book: PRECISE + AI

Selling today gives you a second set of eyes. Most SDRs already record calls. Tools like Otter and Fathom capture Zoom or Teams meetings and turn them into searchable transcripts. The tools will change. The advantage won't.

You can export a transcript, drop it into our AI tool called PRECISECoach, and ask it to evaluate the call against the PRECISE Playbook. AI shows patterns. You still own the truth. Use the Call Book to capture your intent and self-score. Use PRECISECoach to surface blind spots. Paper plus pixels beats either one alone.

"Tom, You're About to Be Fired"

If this still sounds theoretical, that's fine. Now let's ruin that.

Tom was the rep everyone liked but nobody feared on a leaderboard. Great attitude. Upbeat. Nervous on calls. He talked too much, bounced between topics, and skipped the process under pressure.

One day his manager called me. "Sully, we're about to fire Tom."

I wasn't surprised. I said, "Give me one month. I'll travel with him once a week and coach him up on how to use the selling skills we taught him. If he doesn't improve after that one month, you can let him go."

"What can you fix in a month?" the manager asked.

"Probably nothing," I said. "But give me a shot."

That same day, I took the seven steps that would become PRECISE, dropped them into a simple Word document, printed them at Kinko's, and made the first PRECISE Call Book.

The First Wednesday

I met Tom for at a coffee shop in downtown Chicago. We sat down, small talked for a few minutes and I hit him with:

"Tom, you're about to be fired."

He went pale. "Really?"

"Look at your numbers. You haven't made monthly quota in almost a year," I said.

After a long pause, he asked, "What do I do?"

I slid the call book in front of him and said, "You follow this book," I said. "Every call. Every time." Before you walk into each call, look at it. Let those steps come off the pages and into your brain. Then use it as a notepad to keep you on track during the call. Then after the call, use it to evaluate your performance.

Before our first call that day, I stopped him at the door. "Grab your book. If you get lost, look down."

The call was awful. He talked too much. Asked almost no questions. Jumped to features. Missed the close completely.

Back in the car, I said, "Grade yourself."

He read each PRECISE Action and shook his head. "Nope." "Nope." "Butchered that."

The sheet did the coaching for me.

Watching the Pages Change

The next Wednesday, his Call Book was already open—filled with handwriting, circles, arrows, and painful honesty.

Patterns jumped off the page: "Jumped to features too early." "Forgot CLEAR questions." "Didn't confirm next step."

We made more calls. Still choppy. Still awkward. But different.

Week after week, the notes changed. His posture changed. He stopped gripping the steering wheel like a life raft. He sounded calmer, more curious, more in control.

He wasn't winging it anymore. He was running a process.

Day 20: The Breakthrough

On day twenty, it clicked.

Before the call, Tom walked through his objective out loud, glanced at his Call Book, and took a breath. Inside the meeting, he executed what he'd been practicing: Respect first. Questions before features. Calm under indecision. A clear next step.

We walked out with a $50,000 equipment order. Tom was so pumped he walked down the medical office hallway looking for the first pharmaceutical rep he could find to chest bump!

He grabbed his Call Book, flipped to a fresh page, grabbed his pen and went down the list on his call sheet. "Prepared—yes." "Respect & Trust—yes." "CLEAR questions—yes." "One thing to improve..."

Then he slid the book to me. "Any feedback?"

I smiled. "Nope."

From Last Place to #1

That call needed no tweaking. On that day, Day 20, I had witnessed the best demo meeting I had seen after traveling and coaching sales reps all across the country. That day, Tom had become his company's top performer...in **20 Days!**

Tom didn't change his personality. He changed his habits.

Within months, he was leading the company in equipment sales.

About a year later after consistently dominating, he called me. "Sully, I got an offer from Medtronic. And they are going to pay be twice as much as I am making at Welch Allyn."

My first reaction was, "You son of a bitch!"

My second reaction was, "Damn, do they have any other open sales territories?"

Now armed with a repeatable playbook and the hunger to be a top performer, Tom went on to have an amazing career in sales.

What This Means for You

Tom's story isn't about luck. It's about a rep who stopped winging it and committed to telling himself the truth—one call at a time.

You can do the same thing. Plan the call. Run the call. Evaluate the call. Use AI if you want—but never outsource ownership.

Commit to this for 20 days. Top performers don't guess. They don't hope. They don't wing it. They review the tape. They adjust. They get better on purpose.

Stay PRECISE with your inputs, and the outcomes will take care of themselves. And one day, you'll realize you're not just surviving in sales anymore. You're leading the board.

Because here's what Tom learned—and what you're about to learn:

The reps who win aren't the ones with the best territory, the easiest product, or the most natural charisma.

They're the ones who commit to a process and refuse to wing it.

You've got the process.

Now go be relentless about using it.

The work begins now.

A Tuesday Morning at PRECISE

This is not a special day. This is a Tuesday.

Every principle in this book was built to be used. Not discussed. Not bookmarked. Not agreed with over coffee and forgotten by lunch. Used. So before you close this book and decide what to do with what you just read, I want to show you what it looks like when a team actually runs this system. Not a case study from five years ago. Not a sanitized success story. A single Tuesday morning inside my company.

At 10:30 AM, I posted a message to my SDR team. It said what I always say: judge your day by the number of meetings you booked, not the number of hours you put in. Four hours and zero meetings is not a successful day. Six hours and zero meetings is more acceptable because at least you showed you were working, not watching the clock. But two hours and two meetings? Nobody cares about the other six. The best reps I have ever worked with rush to the finish line and blow through it. And if they fall short, they put in the extra work to get there. PRECISE teaches clients how to outwork and outperform everybody. We don't live by average standards.

Four minutes later, the first meeting came in.

• • •

One of my reps connected with a VP of Sales at a company that works inside the federal government—classified environments, intelligence community, behind-the-green-door buyers. This is not a prospect you reach with a generic pitch. The VP tested him immediately: "Do you actually have the ability to get inside those agencies?" That's not curiosity. That's a credibility test. A rep without training hears that question and gets defensive. My rep heard it and leaned in. He used the CLEAR questioning framework to uncover the real pain: it wasn't rep capability. This VP already had strong closers. His problem was finding qualified buyers in an environment where standard tools don't work. LinkedIn is useless. Spray-and-pray is a career-ender. My rep identified the gap, positioned the solution, and booked a meeting with our senior consultant—all in sixteen minutes.

But here's what separates a trained SDR from someone just dialing for dollars. After the call, my rep posted a full strategic briefing for the team handling the next conversation. Not a name and a phone number. Not "seems interested." A detailed breakdown of the prospect's sales philosophy, his real pain points, his industry constraints, his objections—and why those objections were actually buying behavior. He mapped the decision-making landscape before anyone asked him to. That's the Explore method in action. That's posture. That's what this book teaches, and that's what it looks like when someone actually does it.

While that briefing was being posted, another rep booked a meeting in wound care. He reached an Assistant Director of Nursing at a skilled nursing facility in Ohio. Within ten minutes, he had identified the facility's current wound care program, confirmed their patient volume, and mapped the decision-making structure— the ADON handles clinical and day-to-day, the Director of Nursing handles strategic and approval. He didn't just get one of them on the call. He got both to accept the meeting. Two decision-makers confirmed before the call was even cold. His post-call notes distinguished exactly what each stakeholder cares about and how the next conversation should be framed for each of them.

Another rep booked a discovery session with a podiatry practice. Ten chronic wound patients a week. Shared decision-making between the office manager and physicians. He identified the office manager as both gatekeeper and internal champion, noted that she needs clean talking points to bring to the doctors, and recommended framing the demo as informational rather than a sales commitment—because he read the room correctly and knew that reducing perceived risk was the key to getting the next conversation.

A fourth rep booked his third meeting of the morning. Third. While everyone else was warming up, he was already in the construction technology space, setting a meeting with a superintendent at a billion-dollar electrical contractor. Then my team's energy started feeding on itself. Teammates started calling out each other's wins in real time. Not because someone told them to. Because momentum is contagious when it's built on real results, not pep talks.

By the time another rep booked a meeting with a Chief Sales Officer in the cannabis industry—a three-person company where standard lead-gen tools are useless and the founder is the entire sales org—it was 11:25 AM. Five industries. Multiple decision-makers mapped. Strategic briefings written. And the team was still dialing.

· · ·

I am telling you this not to impress you. I am telling you this because it is the answer to the question you are asking yourself right now.

Every reader gets to this point in a book like this and thinks the same thing: "This sounds great, but does it actually work?"

It works at 10:34 on a Tuesday. It works across wound care and cannabis and federal intelligence and senior living and construction. It works when one rep is talking to a VP who manages classified government contracts and another is booking a demo with a nursing home in Shaker Heights, Ohio. It works because the system is the system. CLEAR questioning doesn't care what industry you're in. The Explore method doesn't change based on your product. Posture is posture whether you're calling a three-person startup or a billion-dollar contractor.

My team is not special. They are trained. They run the same framework you just spent twenty days learning. They prepare the same way this book taught you to prepare. They handle objections the same way you practiced handling them. The only difference between my team and most sales floors in America is that my people adopted the system instead of just attending the training.

That's the choice I put in front of you on the back cover of this book. Most sellers will nod, agree, and drift back to what's familiar. A smaller group will adopt new standards and refuse to wing it again.

My team made their choice. They made it again this morning. They'll make it again tomorrow.

Now it's yours.

About the Author

Brian Sullivan, CSP—known to most people as Sully—is the founder of PRECISE Selling, a sales training and performance company that has helped more than 1,200 organizations stop winging important conversations and start leading them with confidence.

A Certified Speaking Professional (CSP)—a designation held by fewer than 7% of professional speakers worldwide—Brian has spent more than three decades in B2B sales, leadership, and training across manufacturing, medical, financial services, distribution, and professional services. His work centers on one core belief: sales success isn't about being louder, slicker, or more aggressive—it's about posture, preparation, and clarity in conversation.

Brian's team doesn't just teach selling—they do it. His PRECISE Performer sales development team makes hundreds of outbound calls daily, carries real quotas, and closes deals using the same system taught in this book. Companies that want expert prospectors and closers working their pipeline can hire PRECISE Performers directly—trained reps who execute the system from day one.

Brian is the co-host of *Golf Underground* on ESPN Kansas City alongside MLB Hall of Famer George Brett, and teaches sales the way it actually happens—on the phone, in meetings, and under pressure.

preciseselling.com

APPENDIX A

PRECISE Call Book Sheets

Print these sheets or keep them open during calls.
Use them to stay on track and evaluate yourself honestly
afterward.

COLD PROSPECTING CALL SHEET (During Call)

Account Name: _____ Date: _____

Tasks	Notes
Preparation: Research/LinkedIn. Meeting Objective	
Respect and Trust: Gatekeeper: "Hoping you could help me. Am following up on an email I sent to _____." Prospect: "Can I have 30 seconds to explain why I called, and then you can decide if it's worth continuing?"	
Engage: Value/Pain/Name-Drop Hook Takeaway: "Called you out of the blue and wasn't sure if you were in need of what we provide." Currently Looked at Enjoy/Effective Alter Responsible for decision	
Convey Solution: Your Company Pitch/Story • Focus on Bullets • Use stories • Use visuals	
Indecision: Stop Hear them out Ask a Question Respond Pack with agreement	
Secure Agreement: "Can you see how this could help?" / "Does this feel worth exploring?" Two-choice: "Would a demo on [date] or [date] be better?"	
Explore: Upsell/Cross-sell and Referrals	
Posture: Enthusiastic, Warm, Smiled, Stood up	
PIC Knowledge: Demonstrated clear knowledge of client, company, solutions	

COLD PROSPECTING CALL SHEET (Post Call)

Account Name: _____   Date: _____

Tasks	Notes
Preparation: Research/LinkedIn. Meeting Objective	
Respect and Trust: Gatekeeper: "Hoping you could help me. Am following up on an email I sent to _____." Prospect: "Can I have 30 seconds to explain why I called, and then you can decide if it's worth continuing?"	
Engage: Value/Pain/Name-Drop Hook Takeaway: "Called you out of the blue and wasn't sure if you were in need of what we provide." Currently Looked at Enjoy/Effective Alter Responsible for decision	
Convey Solution: Your Company Pitch/Story • Focus on Bullets • Use stories • Use visuals	
Indecision: Stop Hear them out Ask a Question Respond Pack with agreement	
Secure Agreement: "Can you see how this could help?" / "Does this feel worth exploring?" Two-choice: "Would a demo on [date] or [date] be better?"	
Explore: Upsell/Cross-sell and Referrals	
Posture: Enthusiastic, Warm, Smiled, Stood up	
PIC Knowledge: Demonstrated clear knowledge of client, company, solutions	

WARM PROSPECT CALL SHEET (During Call)

Account Name: _____ Date: _____

Tasks	Notes
Preparation: Research/LinkedIn. Meeting Objective	
Respect and Trust: • "Thank you for your time." • "I know your time is valuable so I want to make this as quick and as valuable as possible." • "If you believe we have a solution let's talk more. If not, thank you anyway for having me."	
Engage: • "What got you interested in learning more?" • "Have you already decided on the need for a solution like this?" Currently Looked at Enjoy/Effective Alter Responsible for decision	
Convey Solution: Your Company Pitch/Story • Focus on Bullets • Use stories • Use visuals	
Indecision: Stop Hear them out Ask a Question Respond Pack with agreement	
Secure Agreement: "Does this align with what you were hoping to solve?" Three-choice Close: 1) Financial proposal, 2) Involve stakeholder, 3) Deeper demo	
Explore: Upsell/Cross-sell and Referrals	
Posture: Enthusiastic, Warm, Smiled, Stood up	
PIC Knowledge: Demonstrated clear knowledge of client, company, solutions	

WARM PROSPECT CALL SHEET (Post Call)

Account Name: _____   Date: _____

Tasks	Notes
Preparation: Research/LinkedIn. Meeting Objective	
Respect and Trust: • "Thank you for your time." • "I know you time is valuable so I want to make this as quick and as valuable as possible." • "If you believe we have a solution let's talk more. If not, thank you anyway for having me."	
Engage: • "What got you interested in learning more?" • "Have you already decided on the need for a solution like this?" Currently Looked at Enjoy/Effective Alter Responsible for decision	
Convey Solution: Your Company Pitch/Story • Focus on Bullets • Use stories • Use visuals	
Indecision: Stop Hear them out Ask a Question Respond Pack with agreement	
Secure Agreement: "Does this align with what you were hoping to solve?" Three-choice Close: 1) Financial proposal, 2) Involve stakeholder, 3) Deeper demo	
Explore: Upsell/Cross-sell and Referrals	
Posture: Enthusiastic, Warm, Smiled, Stood up	
PIC Knowledge: Demonstrated clear knowledge of client, company, solutions	

APPENDIX B

PRECISE Resources

Scan the QR code or visit the link below to access all PRECISE resources in one place.

preciseselling.com/booklinks

PRECISE Call Sheets

Download printable PDFs of all four sheets so you can save, print, and reuse them with your team:

• Cold Prospecting Call Sheet – During Call

• Cold Prospecting Call Sheet – Post Call

• Warm Prospect Call Sheet – During Call

• Warm Prospect Call Sheet – Post Call

PRECISE Coach

Practice your calls with an AI-powered coach. Upload a transcript or role-play live, and get instant feedback on your PRECISE execution. It's like having a sales manager in your pocket.

Weekly Videos & Community

Follow PRECISE Selling on YouTube, LinkedIn, Instagram, X, Facebook, and TikTok for weekly videos, live call breakdowns, objection handling tips, and conversations with other B2B reps and leaders.

All links available at **preciseselling.com/booklinks**

APPENDIX C

For Sales Leaders

Your reps read the book. Now what?

Handing someone a book and hoping they improve is like giving them a gym membership and expecting muscles. PRECISE only works if you coach it, measure it, and model it yourself.

1. Weekly PRECISE Coaching Rhythm

Run one 10–20 minute team huddle each week focused on a single PRECISE skill (Respect & Trust, CLEAR questions, SHARP for indecision, Three Choice Close).

In 1:1s, review 2–3 recent calls or Call Sheets instead of only talking about the forecast. Coach how they opened, questioned, conveyed, and secured next steps.

2. Activity & Accountability

Choose 2–3 lead indicators you will track for every rep, such as:

• PRECISE Call Sheets completed per week

• New first meetings booked

• CLEAR-driven discoveries completed

Make these visible on a simple dashboard and use them as coaching triggers, not weapons. When numbers dip, schedule extra practice or ride-alongs.

3. How to Use This Book With Your Team

Use the book as a 20-day sprint: one chapter per day, with a short drill at every team meeting.

Ask each rep to bring at least one filled-out Call Sheet to pipeline or 1:1 meetings so you coach behavior, not just results.

4. Lead by Example

Your team watches what you do, not what you say. Use PRECISE language in your own calls. Fill out a Call Sheet after your customer conversations. When they see you running the process, they'll believe it matters.

5. Go Deeper With Your Team

This book gives your team the framework. If you want structured implementation, we offer:

PRECISE Video Training — A full-day e-learning course your team can complete on their own schedule. Every rep gets the same foundation, delivered consistently.

PRECISE Bootcamps — Live, intensive training where we work with your team in real-time on real calls. Every bootcamp participant receives this book, plus hands-on coaching.

PRECISE Performers — We cold call for you. Our trained SDRs use the PRECISE methodology to fill your AEs' calendars with qualified meetings.

Consulting & Custom Training — For organizations that want tailored implementation, ongoing coaching, or help building PRECISE into your sales culture.

Visit **preciseselling.com/booklinks** or contact us directly to talk about what's right for your team.

The Bottom Line

Your job is to create a culture where PRECISE is used every day—on call sheets, in meetings, and in coaching.

Do that, and the numbers will follow.

www.ingramcontent.com/pod-product-compliance
Lightning Source LLC
Chambersburg PA
CBHW030410130626
46549CB00004B/1706